Berlitz®
Turkey

Front cover: Antalya

Right: Mevlâna Tekkesi, Konya

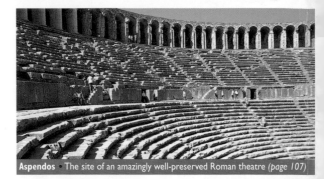

Aspendos • The site of an amazingly well-preserved Roman theatre *(page 107)*

Gaziantep Archaeological Museum
• Hundreds of square metres of vivid Roman mosaics, the best in the Middle East, form the heart of this astonishing collection *(page 122)*

Blue Mosque • Its interior is aglow with thousands of decorated tiles *(page 30)*

Hagia Sophia •
Completed in AD537, it ranks among the wonders of the world *(page 28)*

Pamukkale • Mineral-rich springs formed its irresistible travertine terraces *(page 80)*

Ephesus • Its Roman ruins are the most extensive in the Mediterranean *(page 75)*

Patara • Turkey's longest continuous beach, its dunes romantically encroaching on the ruins of an ancient city *(page 98)*

Ölüdeniz • Pine-clad hills and white-sand beaches back the turquoise waters of this beautiful stretch of coastline *(page 93)*

Topkapı Palace • Centuries of Ottoman pomp and power are on display *(page 34)*

Nemrut Dağı • Huge stone heads stare from a mountaintop in the Mesopotamian basin *(page 124)*

A PERFECT TOUR

Days 1–2 İstanbul

Enter Topkapı Palace early, then see Aya Sofya and the Blue Mosque. Have lunch nearby before strolling west via the Grand Bazaar to the Süleymaniye mosque, later descending to the colourful Spice Bazaar. The next day, take a ferry up the Bosphorus, visiting various museums or waterside villas. Return in the evening to sample Beyoğlu's nightlife.

Days 5–6 Ayvalık to Pamukkale

After a morning swim, head down the Aegean coast to Ayvalık, in time for lunch. Explore nearby Pergamon before continuing south to Selçuk. Spend the next morning at Ephesus, then stop at Priene, Miletus or Didyma after lunch. Next head inland to Pamukkale in time for sunset.

Days 7–8 On to Patara

After viewing the terraces and ancient Hierapolis, loop round via Aphrodisias, lunching at adjacent Geyre village, before continuing to Highway 400 en route to Dalyan. Get up early for a river cruise to Kaunos. Then drive east, pausing for lunch at Kaya Köyü, before visiting two sites from among Tlos, Pınara, Xanthos or the Letoön. Arrive at Gelemiş, gateway to Patara beach and ruins.

Days 3–4 Bursa to Assos

Hire a car and take the ferry to Mudanya or Yalova, ports for Bursa. Tour Bursa then set off west for Çanakkale, perhaps making it to Troy before sunset. The following day, cross to Eceabat for the battlefields of Gallipoli. Return to the mainland and head for Assos, watching the sunset over Lésvos from the acropolis before dinner.

OF TURKEY

Day 11 — Termessos to Cappadocia

Spend the next morning at Termessos, seeing either Perge or Aspendos before lunch (and a swim) at Side. Then take the inland road via Beyşehir to Konya by nightfall. Having paid your respects to the Mevlâna, continue after lunch to Cappadocia, choosing Ürgüp or Göreme as a base.

Days 9–10 — Kaş to Antalya

Having enjoyed Patara, continue east to Kaş for lunch, then drive early in the afternoon to Kekova, where boatmen take you to Simena and other local highlights. Next day, continue east, pausing at Demre for ancient Myra, before swimming and lunch at Çıralı. Catch Phaselis ruins before they close, then arrive at Antalya's old town.

Day 14 — Ankara

Drive to Ankara, hand in the rental car, then tour the city's highlights on foot. The Hisar (Castle), copper bazaar and Museum of Anatolian Civilisations are all well worth a visit and just a few paces apart.

Days 12–13 — Cappadocia

In one day it is possible to comfortably visit the Göreme Open-Air Museum; plus the distinctive villages of Üçhisar, Ortahisar and Ürgüp with their cave dwellings, churches and stunning views; as well as the underground city at Avanos. On Day 13, take in Sinasos, the underground city at Derinkuyu, and a walk in the Ihlara Valley.

CONTENTS

26

124

68

Features

16

42

137

INTRODUCTION

Today, Turkey is one of the world's favourite holiday playgrounds, and this land that bridges Europe and Asia has accommodated a stampede of travellers for millennia (although many of the earlier visitors came dressed in armour and had conquest and plunder on their minds). To experience the richness of this nation you need only follow paths well beaten since ancient times. Since the earliest prehistoric cultures of Anatolia this has been the crossroads of civilisations: the Hittites, Greeks, Persians, Romans, Byzantines, Seljuks, Crusaders, Mongols, Ottomans, French, British and Italians have all passed through and left their imprint on this most complex and beautiful of societies.

In İstanbul, climb the staircase outside the waterfront entrance to the Egyptian Bazaar and you will find yourself in the Rüstem Paşa Camii, a gem of a mosque designed by the great Ottoman architect Sinan and awash with magnificent İznik tiles. At Termessos, on the Mediterranean coast, scramble up a steep mountain path and before you lies an ancient Greek theatre perched spectacularly on the edge of a precipice. In the Ihlara Valley in Cappadocia, insignificant holes in the cliff open out into jewel-like cave-churches rich in glorious Byzantine frescoes. In Antakya, another cave-church is, astoundingly, where saints Peter, Paul and Barnabas gathered in secret to create and name their new religion – Christianity.

Of the many fabulous experiences that await you in Turkey, one well worth seeking out is the pleasure of swimming from beaches at Patara, Olympos, Side or Phaselis, raising your head from the warm Mediterranean waters, and

A beautifully decorative tile found in Topkapı Palace, İstanbul

looking back towards a shore littered with the remains of ancient, once-thriving cities: a ruined temple here, a granary there, a bath complex rising from the scrub. Or there's the unsettling sensation of looking over the side of a boat gliding over the waters of the Kekova Sound to see Roman mosaics and columns glistening beneath the surface.

Size and Landscape

Geographically, Turkey is huge, with 7,200km (4,500 miles) of coast, and land frontiers with Armenia, Azerbaijan, Bulgaria, Georgia, Greece, Iran, Iraq and Syria. The border between Europe and Asia runs through the middle of İstanbul, along the Bosphorus, one of the most strategically important waterways in the world.

The country's landscape is as varied as it is huge. Sculpted cliffs, punctuated by golden beaches and lapped by in-

Mount Ararat

digo and turquoise seas, line the Aegean and Mediterranean coasts, their valleys a sea of greenhouses producing, among many other things, some of the most delicious tomatoes in the world. A little way inland, valleys give way to rocky mountains clad in pine forests, their lower slopes filled with orchards that flutter with pink and white blossoms in spring. Behind the mountains stretch the vast rolling grasslands of the Anatolian plateau with its fiercely hot summers and bitterly cold winters.

In the southeast, ancient Mesopotamia (the Near East), so famed for its fertility that some claim it to be the original Garden of Eden, lies between the Euphrates and Tigris rivers. The government has created a vast network of dams based on the two rivers, to generate hydroelectricity and irrigate the semi-desert to the southeast – great for Turkey, not so good for the desert countries to the south, for whom the rivers are, quite literally, a lifeline, or for the Kurds, some of whom claim the region as an independent state.

In the border territories of the far east, the mountains again soar skywards, culminating in the massive bulk of Mount Ararat, Turkey's highest peak at 5,137m (16,853ft). This, according to legend, is the last resting place of Noah's Ark. Beyond this region lie the steppes of Central Asia, from where several waves of invaders have arrived to shape Turkey's people and culture.

Atatürk's Legacy

There is a famous Turkish saying, coined like so much in Turkey by Kemal Atatürk, *'Ne mutlu Türküm diyene!'* (Happy is he who calls himself a Turk.) There are few countries as patriotic, but astonishingly, Turkey as it exists today has been a country for less than 100 years, carved by Atatürk from the wreckage of the Ottoman Empire at the end of World War I. He was building a nation and needed to create an identity that would bring people together. The Ottomans were discredited, seen as cruel and decadent rulers, so he looked further back into history and settled on the Turks, who began arriving in the Anatolian peninsula during the 11th century AD. Yet relatively few people in Turkey today are ethnically Turkish; people are far more likely to admit to Circassian, Bosnian, Bulgarian, Greek or Albanian ancestry, a consequence of the Ottoman Empire's rapid collapse from the early 19th century onwards.

Atatürk also endowed the country with one of the world's most progressive constitutions – a democratic, strictly secular, republican form of government – and one of the world's largest standing armies. For decades, the two reinforced each other. The army, which idolises Atatürk even more than the general populace, sees itself as the guardian of his legacy. It has stepped in three times in bloodless coups to remove ostensibly unsuitable governments, whether incompetent or overtly sectarian. A religious party that won an election and took power in 1997 was banned and its government toppled. While a religious party again holds office, it does so under the implicit understanding that it would not attempt to introduce religious law.

People and Religion

The vast bulk of the population is Muslim, either Sunni or Alevi. Islam in Turkey is generally an open, welcoming brand of the religion. The visitor is made to feel at home and the secular, emancipated society created by Atatürk is still clearly visible in contemporary culture and both men's and women's fashions. The muezzin's call to prayer competes with honking horns and pop music blaring from hundreds of sound systems; the object of the age-old ritual of bargaining is as likely to be a mobile phone or cheap watch as it is a bag of spices or a kilim. Even those young İstanbul women who have adopted the headscarf may well have chosen a colourful designer version that highlights rather than conceals what is beneath.

Turkey nurtures many subcultures within its borders. İstanbul, İzmir and Ankara have a sophisticated international lifestyle; a casual, beachfront charm typifies the coastal resorts. Yet go only a few kilometres inland and you see an entirely different country, peopled by chickens and goats, squat women in headscarves, cardigans and baggy trousers, and men with voluptuous moustaches and flat caps. This is a country where women work the fields, a flock of small children tugging at their clothes, while the men hang out in tea shops playing backgammon and righting the ills of the world.

Young faces of Turkey

A staging-point for armies and empires throughout its history, Turkey still walks the delicate tightrope between East and West, looking for friends and influence in both directions, and acting as a moderate buffer zone in the current tense political atmosphere. So far, it has succeeded admirably.

A BRIEF HISTORY

At ancient Troy, myth and historical evidence suggest that three millennia ago the Greek Odysseus rolled a large wooden horse through the city gates as a gift. The rest of the story is told in the *Iliad*: soldiers crept out of the horse under cover of darkness, overpowered Troy's defenders and freed Helen, whose face, it is said, launched a thousand ships. Nearby, at Gallipoli, more than 250,000 troops on both sides were killed or wounded during fighting in 1915. At Pergamon and Ephesus, farther south along the Aegean coast, great libraries attracted the ancient world's scholars. And in Constantinople/İstanbul, at Konya and at Edirne, the Byzantines, Seljuks and Ottomans established their respective empires.

With so many events having unfolded across its coasts, plains and mountains, Turkey is rich in tales of conquest and glory, and the landscape is strewn with the remains of the places where these events transpired. For much of its long history Turkey has been at or near the centre of the world.

Conquerors and the Conquered

In around 9000BC, Palaeolithic peoples were painting caves at Belbaşı and Beldibi near Antalya. By 6250BC, flourishing towns existed. Çatalhöyük, south of Konya, is considered the second-oldest known town (after Jericho). It had a population of around 5,000, and is the first place in the world to have used irrigation and domesticated sheep and pigs. Other, as yet unexcavated and possibly older settlements are known to exist nearby.

By the 2nd millennium BC, written history was in the making. In the west, Troy was already 1,000 years old. The Hittites crossed the Caucasus to establish a stronghold in central Anatolia, leaving behind them sites such as Boğazköy

(Hattuşa), Yazılıkaya, Alacahöyük and Karatepe, south of Ankara. After the collapse of the Hittite civilisation in the 13th century BC, successive waves of colonists arrived from the Balkan peninsula until about 800BC. The Phrygians moved down from Thrace, taking over most of central and western Turkey. Little now remains of their empire, other than the ruined city at Gordion, home to King Midas of the golden touch. The Lydians settled in Sardis, near the Aegean coast, their fortunes reaching a pinnacle under the fabulously rich King Croesus, who invented coins and dice. The wild coast of the southwest Mediterranean was the territory of the Lycians, described by the Hittites as a proudly independent, matriarchal society. The people of Xanthos twice took this desire for independence to extremes, preferring mass suicide to surrender to Persians and Romans in turn. As Greek city-states took root around the coast from Pergamon to As-

Hattuşa, the ancient Hittite capital in Anatolia

pendos, theatres, temples, colonnaded agoras and bathhouses appeared. Wealth was spurred by growing international trade, both east to Asia and west to Europe.

This affluent society tempted envious outsiders, and in 546BC the Persians, led by Cyrus II, swept west from Persepolis, conquering much of Anatolia. Their hegemony was only broken in 334BC by the next great imperialist, Alexander the Great, who conquered territory as far as India. Over the next two centuries, the original cultures and languages of ancient Anatolia were gradually engulfed by Hellenistic civilisation.

In 133BC, King Attalos III of Pergamon left his kingdom to the Romans. From this toehold, the Romans expanded rapidly, unifying the many city-states and kingdoms of Anatolia as the province of Asia Minor. With the Romans came the relative calm and prosperity of the *pax romana*, although the 3rd century AD saw violent invasions by the Goths and Persians.

Pergamon

Early Christians

Southeastern Turkey had long been integral to Biblical history; Abraham lived at Harran and Noah's Ark is said to have grounded on Mount Ararat. From the 1st century AD, Christianity began taking hold across the Roman Empire. In Antakya (Antioch), saints Peter, Paul

and Barnabas first founded
and named the Christian religion. St Paul, brought up in
Tarsus as Saul the tax col-
lector before his blinding
revelation on the road to
Damascus, followed an itin-
erary that may well be the

envy of a modern traveller, preaching at Alexandria Troas,
Assos, Ephesus, Patara, Myra and elsewhere in Asia Minor.
St John the Evangelist settled in Ephesus, allegedly in the
company of the Virgin Mary. The early Christian inhabitants
of Cappadocia found that the cave-riddled landscape was
ideally suited to hermetic monasticism and to the construction of simple underground churches, of which more than
600 continue to impart a sense of spirituality.

From AD312 onwards, Emperor Constantine strongly
favoured Christianity, although he himself only converted on
his deathbed. Constantine dispatched his mother, Helena
(later made a saint), to the Holy Land where she conveniently
identified Christ's place of execution and tomb, and returned
home with large numbers of relics, including enough of the
True Cross to build a boat. By 325, Christianity had splin-
tered into so many heretical factions that Constantine was
forced to call a conference in Nicaea (modern İznik), which
laid down the basic tenets of the faith, the Nicene Creed.

Meanwhile, the western part of the empire was under increasing pressure from invading barbarians. Between 322 and
330, Constantine moved from Rome to his new capital, Constantinople, built around an old Greek fishing port, Byzantium. The empire split into independently ruled eastern and
western halves a few decades after Constantine's death in 337.
The western portion, still ruled from Rome, but starved of re-
sources, limped on until its demise in AD476.

Hagia Sophia mosaic

Byzantines and Seljuks

The eastern (Byzantine) empire by contrast flourished. Constantinople grew ever more splendid, with vast palaces and great churches, of which the finest was Hagia Sophia, built by Emperor Justinian, and still standing today. However the imperial frontiers were repeatedly tested, by the Slavs in the west, the Avars from Central Asia and the Sassanid Persians in the southeast. In 647, Islamic religion entered Anatolia in the form of Arab warriors who reached the gates of Constantinople in 673 before being repulsed – after a four-year siege. A second attack in 717–18 took most of the empire's eastern provinces. Islam brought a new civilisation, religion, language and script. Christians were tolerated, but held inferior civil status and paid more tax – good incentives to convert. Some Christians espoused iconoclasm, replacing the faces on many frescoes and mosaics with geometric motifs. Under the Macedonian dynasty, inaugurated in 867, icon-worship was restored and the fightback began, but it was 1018 before the Byzantines recovered all their possessions.

Within decades, there was a new threat in the form of the Seljuks, who traced their origins to the Asian steppes. In 1071, at the Battle of Manzikert, they routed the Byzantine Army, capturing the emperor. From their capital in Konya, the Seljuks expanded their Sultanate of Rum at the expense of the Byzantine Empire. Ruins of the *kervansarays* (inns), bridges and roads they built across their holdings to accommodate increased trade along the Silk Route attest to their immense but short-lived power. They were toppled by the 13th-century Mongol invasions of Genghis Khan.

In both northeast Anatolia and southerly Cilicia, the Armenians took advantage of Byzantine weakness to carve out semi-independent states after the late 11th century. From the west, Christian Europe marched east on a holy crusade against the Muslim infidel. Byzantine land was decimated by the passing armies, while the western invaders also set up Latin principalities in Antioch, Edessa and Jerusalem. In 1204, the Fourth Crusade did not bother to attack the Muslims of the Holy Land, but instead ransacked Constantinople and set up a new Latin Empire. The Byzantine emperors, who fled to Nicaea, only recovered their city in 1261.

Crusaders sack Constantinople

Enter the Ottomans

The Ottomans first appeared as a local clan who helped the Seljuks defeat a Mongol detachment in the 1220s and were given land near Eskişehir in central Anatolia in gratitude. But they gradually took over the Seljuk Empire and, over the next 200 years or so, one sultan after another planted the Ottoman standard on new territories. In 1402, the Mongols reappeared under Timur, and temporarily checked the Ottoman advance by defeating Sultan

Beyazit I. But in 1453, Mehmet II finally conquered Constantinople, renaming it İstanbul and breaking ground for an opulent new palace, the Topkapı.

By 1520, Selim I had brought Palestine, Egypt and Syria under Ottoman control, and imposed Sunni orthodoxy as the state religion, with the caliphate relocated to İstanbul. Between 1520 and 1566, the Ottoman Empire reached its zenith under Süleyman the Magnificent, who doubled the size of the empire, adding lands from northern Africa and Iraq to the Balkans and Hungary. He was also an able administrator and, with the help of his architect Sinan, built some of the empire's greatest monuments. Unfortunately, he was not as wise in his choice of a favourite wife. Roxelana was an ambitious former concubine who convinced the sultan to murder his son Mustafa; her own son Beyazit; and Ibrahim Paşa, his son-in-law, grand vizier (prime minister) and closest advisor – all to promote the succession of her useless first-born son, Selim.

Decline and Fall

Selim II, known to history as 'the Sot', drowned drunk in his bath, but not before the Ottomans suffered their first significant naval defeat at Lepanto in 1571 – though they conquered Cyprus earlier the same year, and retook North Africa in 1578. But under further unenlightened and often debauched sultans, the empire began to crumble. By 1792, the Ottomans had lost most of their European holdings, and by the early 19th century the empire was powerless to prevent Serbia, Greece, Egypt and other territories from declaring independence. The Janissaries, originally a praetorian guard of Christian slave-recruits fanatically dedicated to the sultan, became far too powerful; in 1826, Sultan Mahmut II used loyal forces to massacre them.

At the same time, Europe exerted increasing pressure on the 'sick man of Europe', occasioning numerous, often ineffectual reforms by later sultans. In 1853–6, the Ottomans were saved from Russian domination by siding with the French and British during the Crimean War. Despite increased commercial development and the adoption of some western models in education, the military and the civil service, decline continued through the 19th century. The first effective challenge to Sultan Abdülhamid's autocratic power came from the Committee for Union and Progress (CUP), whose 1908 revolution led to the re-opening of parliament and restoration of the liberal 1876 constitution.

Süleyman the Magnificent

These reforms failed to stop further Ottoman losses during the Balkan Wars of 1912–13 and World War I, in which Turkey sided with the Central powers, and the Anatolian peninsula became one of the main charnel-houses of the conflict. Out of a population of about 21 million, civilian Ottoman victims of disease, slaughter and starvation included approximately 1 million Armenians, 500,000 Greek Orthodox, 500,000 Syriac Christians and 2 million Muslim Turks; the Ottoman armies suffered nearly 800,000 fatalities.

Birth of a Nation

During 1919, the victorious British, French, Greeks and Italians moved in to carve up what was left of the Ottoman Empire; the Greek landing at Smyrna/Izmir in particular goaded hitherto passive Turks into action. Mustafa Kemal, a popular Ottoman general, rallied a resistance movement which ratified the so-called National Pact, declaring the minimum acceptable borders of an independent Turkey; in April 1920 the so-called Nationalists convened the first Grand National Assembly. Over the three-year course of a bloody, see-saw war, the Nationalists under Kemal halted or co-opted the French and Italians and finally in late summer 1922 crushed the Greek expeditionary armies, who retreated in disorder.

In November 1922 the Grand National Assembly abolished the sultanate. On 24 July 1923, the Treaty of Lausanne was ratified, recognising the frontiers won by the Nationalist armies, and completely nullifying the Allied-imposed Treaty of Sèvres from 1920, which had provided for an independent Armenia and Kurdistan. Another Lausanne clause stipulated population exchanges: nearly 1.5 million Anatolian Greek Orthodox, and 400,000 Muslims resident in Greece, switched homelands.

Kemal, now president of the new Turkish Republic, oversaw successive secularist reforms. Polygamy was banned, education for women made mandatory, the fez and turban prohibited, the caliphate abolished, dervish orders outlawed,

Father of the Nation

Born in the now-Greek northern Aegean port of Salonica in 1881, Mustafa Kemal Atatürk had a glittering military career, in spite of early revolutionary tendencies, but really made his reputation during World War I when he took over the defence of Gallipoli, beating off the Allied attack. He then led the revolution that led the country to victory in the War of Independence, established a republic in place of the sultanate and became its first president, secularising the state, liberating women and westernising the nation. He died from cirrhosis of the liver, on 10 November 1938, at the age of only 57, at the Dolmahbaçe Palace, İstanbul.

the Muslim lunar calendar
replaced with the Georgian
calendar, and Arabic script
replaced with a modified
Latin alphabet. Surnames,
once informal, were made
obligatory; Kemal took as his
Atatürk (Father Turk).

Into the Present

After strict economic autarky,
political stagnation and self-
imposed isolation during the
1930s and World War II,
Turkey found – in 1946,
when Russian threats were

Atatürk

renewed – a sponsor in the USA. Massive American aid poured
into the country, which joined NATO in 1952, and the first
multiparty elections were won by Adnan Menderes' opposition Democrat Party. Menderes oversaw improvements to
rural living conditions while encouraging private enterprise
and more religious freedom, but at the cost of economic in-
stability and the antagonism of the urban secularist elite – plus
the armed forces. He was overthrown in 1960 by the first of
several military coups; the army has always viewed itself as
the guarantor of Atatürk's secular legacy, guarding it against
economic and social disorder. After 1960, unstable civilian
regimes presided over a chaotic society, punctuated by Turkey's
invasion of Cyprus in 1974 and a harsh coup in 1980.

Since the definitive return to civilian rule in 1983 under tech-
nocrat Turgut Özal, Turkey has made astonishing progress,
although industrialisation, vastly improved infrastructure and
a place at the G20 top table have come in tandem with peri-
odic high unemployment, corruption, continued para-state

violence against dissidents, a chequered human rights record, hyperinflation and urban terrorist attacks by al-Qaeda affiliates or Kurdish separatists. From 1984 onwards the army confronted a full-bore insurrection in the east by the Kurdish PKK organisation, which is still active along the eastern borders, prompting recent incursions by the army into northern Iraq.

The secularist edifice began to crumble – quite literally – with a catastrophic August 1999 earthquake in northwestern Turkey, in which nearly 40,000 died. The army was upbraided for poor handling of the emergency and Greek rescue teams were the first foreigners on the scene, leading to a sustained rapprochement between the two nations. A severe 2001 economic crash preceded landmark 2002 elections, won decisively by an Islamist party, AK, who formed the first non-coalition government in decades – repeating this feat twice, in 2007 and 2011.

Turkey had been a European Union membership candidate since 1999, but only under AK has it adopted necessary significant reforms. Accession talks began in 2005, but continued Turkish occupation of northern Cyprus (plus opposition from many European countries) remain major stumbling blocks. Enthusiasm for EU membership has waned as doubters tout the

Flag over Topkapı

advantages of being instead a regional power with orientation eastwards. Although the country is polarised between a pro-AK hinterland and a staunchly secularist west coast and Thrace, multiparty democracy is not in imminent danger, the economy avoided the worst of the 2008 crash, tourism roars along and and Turkish pride remains unwavering.

Historical Landmarks

6500BC Neolithic peoples settle near Konya.

1100BC First Greek colonies on Aegean coast.

800BC Phrygian, Lydian and Lycian cultures begin to flourish.

546BC Persians, under Cyrus II (the Great), invade.

334BC Alexander the Great defeats the Persians.

130BC Romans create province of Asia Minor.

AD40 St Paul begins preaching Christianity.

325 Constantine convenes first ecumenical council at Nicaea.

330 Constantinople becomes capital of eastern Roman Empire.

1071 Seljuks enter Anatolia.

1204 Crusaders sack Constantinople.

14th century Rise of the Ottomans begins.

1453 Mehmet II conquers Constantinople, ending Byzantine Empire.

1520–66 Reign of Süleyman the Magnificent.

1683–1792 Ottomans lose much of their European territory.

1839–76 First systematic reform of the Ottoman Empire.

1912–13 Ottomans lose remaining European territories in Balkan Wars.

1914–18 Turks fight in World War I as one of the Central Powers.

1919–1922 War of Independence against Greece, Italy, France.

1923 Turkish Republic is established, with Atatürk as president.

1924–38 Atatürk imposes secularisation and modernisation.

1950 First free elections, won by Adnan Menderes.

1960 Menderes deposed by first military coup.

1974 Turkey invades northern Cyprus.

1983 Return to civilian rule under Turgut Özal.

1984 PKK launches guerilla insurrection in southeast.

1999 Earthquake kills tens of thousands in northwestern Turkey.

2002 Islamist AK Party forms majority government.

2005 Negotiations begin on Turkey joining the EU.

2007 Second AK electoral victory.

2008 Ergenekon conspiracy trial commences.

2011 AK wins again; majority insufficient for drafting a new constitution.

WHERE TO GO

Mosques, minarets, bazaars stacked high with spices, ancient ruins lapped by turquoise waters, churches aglow with frescoes – the mere mention of Turkey launches a seemingly endless stream of exotic images, few living up to the splendour of reality. Nowhere does the cultural wealth of this nation that straddles Europe and Asia come to light more vividly than in İstanbul, the city that bestrides both continents.

İSTANBUL

Its name, according to some, comes from the Greek *eis tin polin*, 'at the city'. There were many centuries when people throughout the world would refer to 'the city'; everyone knew they were talking about this fascinating metropolis that has been known successively as Byzantium, Constantinople and finally **İstanbul**. The city has witnessed the passing of Greeks and Romans, flowered in the 6th century under the Emperor Justinian, and rose from ruin and neglect during the 15th century, when Ottoman Sultan Mehmet II set about building mosques, monuments and the magnificent Topkapı Palace. In 2010, İstanbul was elected the European Capital of Culture, with many special events to mark the occasion.

The city's stunning setting on the hilly terrain of two continents, bisected by boat-choked waterways, is bound to disorient the newcomer, while the monuments, scents and the omnipresence of the exotic can be overwhelming. İstanbul is a city to savour at leisure, whether it be pausing to catch a glimpse of the minaret-pierced skyline or sitting down with a carpet-dealer for your umpteenth glass of ultra-sweet black tea.

Mosque domes in İstanbul

Begin in the old city, where a staggering wealth of sights are within walking distance, then venture across the Golden Horn on the Galata Bridge into modern Beyoğlu and other sections of this city that sprawls along both sides of the Bosphorus.

Sultanahmet

Set on a small peninsula overlooking the Bosphorus and the Golden Horn, this is the historical centre of the city and was, for over 1,500 years, the heart of the Byzantine and Ottoman empires. Here, you can view some of the city's finest museums, step into some of the world's most hallowed religious structures, wander through royal palaces, view ancient ruins, barter at İstanbul's acclaimed bazaars, dine in a Byzantine cistern and sleep in a finely restored Ottoman house. You can do all this quite comfortably, because Old Stambul is relatively small and easy to navigate on foot.

Hagia Sophia (Aya Sofya)

From the time of its completion under the Emperor Justinian in 537, **Hagia Sophia** (Aya Sofya) or the Church of Holy Wisdom (Tues–Sun 9.30am–5pm, until 7pm in summer; charge) was the largest and most important church in the Christian world. This astonishing building quickly assumed similar stature in the Islamic world when the Ottoman sultans appropriated it as a mosque some nine centuries later, adding the four minarets. In 1936, Atatürk converted the structure to a museum, although Christians and Muslims alike still lay claim to it.

Weeping Column

Hagia Sophia's most popular attraction is the Weeping Column in the north aisle. According to legend, Justinian cured a hangover by resting his forehead on it. Since then, the moisture that gathers on its brass-and marble-clad surface is said to cure many ailments.

Hagia Sophia, dedicated in AD536 and still an overpowering space

Contributing in no small part to the overpowering presence of Hagia Sophia is its dome, which was not eclipsed in size until St Peter's rose in Rome 1,000 years later. In designing the dome, Byzantine architects seemingly accomplished the impossible – the massive structure seems to float over the interior of the church, an illusion created by using hollow bricks made of light, porous clay.

Inside, pride of place undoubtedly belongs to the **mosaics**, many commissioned by Justinian to ensure that his church would be the most splendid in Christendom. In the 16th century, Süleyman the Magnificent, in accordance with Islamic law forbidding representation of man or animal, ordered the mosaics to be covered. Fortunately, the protective plaster inadvertently saved the mosaics for posterity. Ongoing restorations continue to reveal the sheer splendour of these works, many in gold, portraying saints and angels. Two of the most important show the Madonna and Child, and Christ flanked by the Virgin Mary and John the Baptist. For a look at more secular images, walk to the far end of the south gallery, where the 11th-century Empress Zoë improvised a convenient way to portray a succession of husbands – when one would pass on, she would simply have the image of his face replaced with that of his successor. On view for the ages is Zoë's last husband, Constantine IX Monomachos.

The Blue Mosque and Surroundings
In the 16th century Sultan Ahmet I commissioned a mosque within the shadow of Hagia Sophia, designed to rival it. The
B▶ **Sultan Ahmet Camii**, better known as the **Blue Mosque** (best to visit early in the morning) had six minarets, equal to the number adorning the Great Mosque in Mecca. To quell the resulting outrage, Sultan Ahmet was forced to donate a

Visiting Mosques

Mosques are free to enter and typically open to visitors from about 9am until dusk, except at prayer times. You must remove your shoes; leave them by the door or take a bag large enough to carry them with you. Bare arms are forbidden and women must cover their heads. You may borrow a scarf at larger mosques, but it's best to carry your own. Do not disturb or take pictures of people who are praying. On exit, give a small tip to the shoe guard, if there is one, and a donation to the mosque.

Mosques have four crucial architectural elements: a courtyard with a şadırvan (ablutions fountain) for ritual washing before prayer; a mihrab, the niche that points towards Mecca to mark the direction to face when praying; a mimber, the pulpit for sermons; and a minaret, the tower from which the muezzin calls time for prayer (usually taped these days). Women have a separate section, and there may also be an attached medrese (religious school), and an imaret (soup-kitchen/hostel for travellers and dervishes).

The Blue Mosque, designed to rival Hagia Sophia

seventh minaret to Mecca. Entering from Sultanahmet Square, pass through the forecourt and side doors (only the faithful can walk through the massive main portal), and you will find yourself standing beneath a canopy of airy domes. The space is bathed in the light of 260 stained-glass windows and aglow with 20,000 blue İznik tiles (from the ceramics-manufacturing city to the south of İstanbul; *see page 58*).

Several buildings surrounding the mosque once housed shops, alms houses and other establishments that serviced the needs of the faithful. These now include the **Arasta Bazaar**, a good shopping area for crafts, which leads to the **Mozaik Müzesi** (Mosaic Museum; Wed–Mon 9.30am–5pm; charge). This shelters a magnificent stretch of mosaic pavement, once the great hall of Justinian's Byzantine imperial palace. Not uncovered until the mid-20th century, the mosaics are in splendid condition and colourfully depict flora, fauna, scenes from mythology and, with some degree of pomp, the occasional emperor. The nearby **Hünkar Kasrı** (Carpet and Kilim Museum; Tues–Sat 9am–noon and 1–4pm; charge) has a fine collection of historic carpets. Should you be inspired to possess such a carpet for yourself, have a look at the state-run Turkish Handwoven Carpets Exhibition in the **Haseki Hürrem Sultan Hamamı** (Wed–Mon 9.30am–5pm; free), a bathhouse built by Mimar Sinan in 1556 for Roxelana, favourite wife of Süleyman the Magnificent.

Just opposite the Blue Mosque is the **Hippodrome**, site of the 100,000-seat stadium that for much of İstanbul's history hosted chariot races, circuses and other entertainments, as well as mass assemblies and an occasional outburst of public violence. It was here, in 1826, that Sultan Mahmut II oversaw the slaughter of the Janissaries, the dangerously powerful and frequently mutinous royal guard. Little remains of the actual structure, but three monuments continue to grace a large greensward at the centre of what was once the chariot track: the **Yılanlı Sütun** (Serpentine Column), taken from the Temple of Apollo at Delphi; the **Ormetaş** (Knitted Column) of Constantine VII Porphyogenitus, and the **Dikilitaş** (obelisk of Pharaoh Thutmose) that Byzantine Emperor Theodosius I brought from Alexandria in AD390.

The Egyptian obelisk

Under the Byzantine and Ottoman empires, Hagia Sophia and the Blue Mosque were surrounded by the palaces of the powerful elite. On the western edge of the Hippodrome, the 16th-century stone Ibrahim Paşa Sarayı (Ibrahim Paşa Palace) is now home to the furniture, carpets and other holdings of the

Stolen horses

The four bronze horses that once graced the Hippodrome were pillaged by Crusaders on their way home from the Holy Land. They are now inside St Mark's Cathedral in Venice (with replicas on the façade).

Turk ve Islam Eserlei Müzesi (Turkish and Islamic Arts Museum; Tues–Sun 9am–5pm; charge), which provides a satisfying look at Ottoman lifestyles. The tenant for whom the palace is named was a one-time confidant of Süleyman the Magnificent who, like so many, fell out of favour and was strangled.

A little further along the road, the **Yerebatan Sarayı** (Underground Palace or Basilica Cistern; daily 9am–5pm; charge) is one of the many vast water tanks the Byzantines built to ensure that the city would be supplied with fresh water during sieges, often reusing older Greek masonry. Among the latter are two famous blocks with carved Medusa heads, one upside down and one on its side, used as column bases; the columns and elaborate arches reflected in the rippling waters produce an eerily fascinating atmosphere. The space is used for concerts during cultural festivals. The **Binbirdirek Sarnıçı** on nearby Klodfarer Caddesi (the Cistern of 1,001 Columns; daily 8am–midnight for sightseeing; charge refunded if you eat in the restaurant) is an even older 4th-century cistern, with 264 columns – in spite of its name.

Archaeological Museum

Near the Topkapı gate, the **Arkeoloji Müzesi** (Archaeological Museum; all sections Tues–Sun 9.30am–5pm, last admission 4.30pm; a single charge covers all three museums here) will help you put things in perspective. An exhibit on İstanbul history nicely explains the city's Greek, Roman, Byzantine and Ottoman past, and gathered here are prize examples of statuary and other artefacts from Troy, Ephesus, Aphrodisias and the many other important archaeological sites throughout Turkey. The star exhibit is the magnificent Alexander Sarcophagus from Sidon.

The complex also includes the **Eski Şark Eserleri Müzesi** (Museum of the Ancient Orient), which houses some astonishing artefacts, including the world's first surviving peace treaty and the gateway of Babylon. The nearby **Cinili Köşk** (Tiled Pavilion) was built in 1472 as an imperial sports pavilion. It is covered inside in colourful İznik tiles, with other Ottoman ceramics on display.

Topkapı Palace

D ▶ The very stones of the **Topkapı Palace** (Topkapı Sarayı) ooze wealth, pleasure and intrigue. This vast residence and administrative centre of the sultans has seen plenty of all three. It consists of an alluring maze of ornate, jewel-filled state rooms, fountain-cooled gardens, and the famous harem, and is set on a lovely hilltop overlooking the confluence of the Sea of Marmara and the Bosphorus.

The various palace pavilions and living quarters are clustered around four courtyards. Cross the first one, the **Court of the Janissaries**, to reach the ticket office. This large open space was the precinct of an elite corps of guards serving the sultan. They were Christian by birth, recruited as young boys from the Balkans, and trained to be soldiers. Janissaries, however, were far more than a professional army – well educated in Islam and civic affairs, they filled some of the highest posts in the palace, ensuring that the sultan was surrounded by loyal retainers. The Ottoman mint (now a civic museum) is in this courtyard, as is the ancient Byzantine church, Aya Irini Kilisesi (Church of Saint Irene), now used as a concert hall and exhibition space.

After you pass Bâb-i-Selam (Gate of Salvation), you will find yourself in the Second Court. The palace kitchens line one side. A couple of rooms have been reconstructed to give some idea of what it was like as a staff of hundreds prepared meals for the palace's 4,000 residents. The various sculleries and oven rooms now display porcelain and glassware. You will notice a disproportionately large collection of Chinese celadon dinnerware, a court favourite because it allegedly changed colour on contact with poisoned food.

The **Divan-i-Humayun** (Imperial Council Chamber), known as *kubbealti* (literally, beneath the cupola) because of its distinctive cupola-like tower, was where the grand vizier met with the Council of State, more familiarly called the 'divan' because members reclined on the couches that line the walls. These proceedings were sometimes observed by the sultan from behind a screen known as the Eye of the Sultan. The many-domed **Inner Treasury**, one of several halls housing the famed Topkapı treasures, displays an extensive collection of arms and armour.

Entrance to the Harem

The **Harem** is an intriguing warren of apartments and courtyards, incorporating about 400 rooms in all (of which you can visit about 40 on the mandatory guided tour). Life here was neither licentious nor, for most of the inhabitants, particularly enjoyable. However, true to the meaning of the word harem, or forbidden, what transpired here was shrouded in mystery, and residents of the complex had little or no contact with the outside world. Aside from the sultan's mother (the valide sultan) and his official wives, who lived in luxury, the Harem also housed, in conditions akin to slavery, hordes of eunuchs, concubines and ladies-in-waiting.

The Kafes, or Veliaht Dairesi (Golden Cage, Apartment of the Heir-Apparent) was a prison. In it lived brothers and other close male relatives of the sultan who might be in line for the throne. Confined here, they could cause little trouble and, circumspect as their lives were, they were unlikely to have access to any treasonous plots. The practice was an improvement upon the wholesale fratricide in which new sultans once engaged to ensure their place on the throne, but it did not breed good rulers. Much of the Harem, especially the apartments occupied by the valide sultan and the sultan himself, are sumptuously domed and tiled, culminating in the Hünkar Sofrasi (Imperial Hall), where the sultan entertained his preferred visitors.

While the Harem was where intimacies of day-to-day life at the Ottoman court transpired, the Third Court was the sultan's official domain. Here, beyond the Bâb-i-Saadet (Gate of Felicity), he received state visitors in the ornate **Arz Odası** (Audience Chamber) – conversing with them only through the grand vizier, as a sultan did not deign to speak directly to anyone but a high-ranking member of court. The Third Court also houses the **Treasury**, where you can view the palace's lustrous collection of 3.5-kg (8-lb) emeralds, the 84-carat 'Spoonmaker' diamond (so called because a peasant allegedly traded the gem for three spoons), and room after room of other jewels and gaudy jewel-encrusted swords, books and garments. The **Pavilion of the Holy Mantle** houses sacred relics of the Prophet Mohammed (including hairs from his beard) and is therefore a place of great religious importance for Muslims.

Tiled ceiling detail

The **Fourth Court** is the most pleasant and relaxed precinct of the palace, laced with gardens, summer houses and pools. The **Sünnet**

Odasi is a richly tiled pavilion in which young princes were circumcised. The Revan Köskü and Bagdat Köskü are two unusually elaborate kiosks to which sultans would retreat to catch a breeze and look out over the city and waterways below. You can do the same from one of the terraces or in the pleasant restaurant.

The Bazaars to Süleymaniye Camii

Below the palace the workaday waterside neighbourhood of Eminönü bustles with crowds coming and going from the Bosphorus ferries, the Sirkeci railway station and the Galata Bridge. The **Mısır Çarşısı** (Egyptian or Spice Bazaar; Mon–Sat 9am–7pm; free) is just a few steps from the ferry docks. Stacked high with bags of spices, nuts and dried fruits, this market opened for business in the 17th century to generate revenue for the **Yeni Camii** (New Mosque) next

Inside the Egyptian Bazaar

door. The little **Rüstem Paşa Camii**, up a flight of steps in ◀ **E**
front of the waterside entrance to the bazaar, may well be
the most beautiful mosque in İstanbul. The façade and interior are covered entirely in İznik tiles arrayed in a distinctive circular pattern.

The Grand Bazaar

The Egyptian Bazaar is only a fraction of the size of the **Kapalı** ◀ **F**
Carşı (Grand Bazaar; daily 9.30am–7pm; free), where up to
4,000 shops, selling everything from mops to mint-condition
antiques, line a covered warren of 65 streets. The streets between the two covered markets are clogged with vendors'
stalls, handcarts transporting sacks of spices, and all manner of exotic hubbub.

Two recent fires, one in 1954 and another in 1974, came
close to destroying the bazaar, but restorations have retained
the tiles, ironwork and other elements of the original Ottoman
style, including its 18 distinctive fountains. The bazaar grew
from a small warehouse built under Mehmet the Conqueror
in the mid-15th century to support a neighbourhood devoted to commerce, supplied by Turkey's position at the western
end of the fabled Silk Road. Merchants decided to connect
their establishments with arcades, and eventually the huge
complex was gated. It's easy to lose your bearings in the maze
of little lanes and hard to escape without buying something.
Some particularly interesting precincts are the Old Bazaar, at
the centre of the complex, where dealers specialise in antiques
and fine jewellery, and the Old Book Bazaar, which is outside
the main market and just to the west.

Beyazit District and Süleymaniye Camii

Just to the west of the main entrance is Beyazit Square. The
forum of the Byzantine Emperor Theodosius, built in
AD393, once stood here, as did a wooden palace occupied

The Süleymaniye Camii at sunset, from Eminönü

by Mehmet the Conqueror before he moved his court to Topkapı Palace. Mehmet later used the old palace as a retirement
home for elderly ladies of his harem. On the south side are
the somewhat austere buildings of **İstanbul University**, formerly the Ottoman War Ministry.

The **Süleymaniye Camii** (tombs 5.30–8pm), just north of
the university, is the largest mosque in İstanbul, situated high
on a hill overlooking the Golden Horn. Considered to be the
highest achievement of Mimar Sinan, Süleyman the Magnificent's master architect, it is austerely beautiful, with a vast
dome supported by four columns and elegant proportions
that lend a spiritual air to the space. Süleyman, his wife Roxelana and Sinan are all buried in the grounds.

The streets immediately to the west of Süleymaniye Camii
lie in the shadow of the **Aqueduct of Valens**, begun in the
4th century as part of the extensive system of reservoirs, cisterns and waterways that supplied the city. A little further

west is the enclave of Fatih (meaning 'the Conqueror'). The Fatih monument commemorates the conquest of İstanbul by Mehmet II in 1453. He is buried next to the **Fatih Camii** (Victory Mosque), the first mosque to rise above Ottoman İstanbul. The original structure and its attendant schools and alms houses were levelled in a 1776 earthquake and, while the mosque that stands in its place has never been completed (the interior is largely undecorated), it is the centre of a large and devout religious community.

The Golden Horn

This fabled waterway is a fjord-like inlet separating the old and new cities. At the far end (easily reached by ferry from the Galata Bridge) is one of the most hallowed sights in Islam. Only Mecca, Medina and Jerusalem are more visited by pilgrims than the **Eyüp Camii** (tomb Tues–Sun 9.30am–4.30pm except at prayer times; donations), burial place of Eyüp Al-Ansari, the standard bearer of the Prophet Mohammed, who was killed carrying the Islamic banner during the 7th-century Arab siege of Constantinople. His tomb was

Mimar Sinan, Master Architect

Mimar Sinan (1489–1588) was the greatest of all Ottoman architects. Born into an Armenian Christian family in a village near Kayseri, he was selected for Janissary training and worked his way through the ranks to become a military engineer before being appointed architect to the Darüs-Saadet (Abode of Felicity) by Süleyman the Magnificent in 1536. Over the next 50 years, he was involved in the design and construction of 34 palaces, 79 mosques, 33 hamams, 19 tombs, 55 schools, 12 kervansarays, 16 külliyeler (charitable institutions) and 7 medreses. He regarded the Selimiye Camii in Edirne (near the Greek border) as his masterpiece; others suggest that the Süleymaniye Camii in İstanbul was greater.

already a revered monument when Mehmet the Conqueror built the mosque in the 15th century. Rebuilt in 1800 after an earthquake, the mosque and tile-covered tomb are reached by a series of peaceful, shaded courtyards. For centuries Ottoman sultans were crowned here and the tombs of many Ottoman notables surround the complex. For a fabulous city view, a cable car leads from here up the hill to the **Pierre Loti Café**.

Nearby, the **Sveti Stefan Bulgar Kilisesi** (Church of Saint Stefan of the Bulgars; admission only by caretaker), once at the centre of the thriving local Bulgarian community, is also one of the most unusual structures in the city. Constructed entirely of cast iron, the church was actually built in Vienna in 1870 and shipped in pieces to İstanbul on more than 100 barges.

Directly west are two remarkable remnants of the Byzantine era. The city's western boundaries are entirely walled in,

Frescoes of saints in the Kariye Müzesi

from the Golden Horn to the Sea of Marmara, with the **fortifications** started by Theodosius II in 413. When the walls were destroyed by an earthquake in 447, a workforce of more than 65,000 civilians rebuilt them in just two months, barely completing the job before the legions of Attila the Hun reached the city and were successfully repelled.

The former Monastery of St Saviour in Chora, now known as the **Kariye Müzesi** (Thur–Tues 9am–5pm; charge), is practically within sight of the walls. Its magnificent mosaics and frescoes were created by Grand Logethete Theodore Metochites in 1316–21. Considered to be among the world's finest surviving examples of Byzantine art, they present a detailed, highly emotional account of the life of Christ.

The **Rahmi M Koç Museum** (Hasköy Caddesi; Tues–Fri 10am–5pm, Sat–Sun 10am–7pm; charge) housed in an old iron foundry on the south side of the Golden Horn is a fascinating private collection of anything involving science, technology and transport, from an 1898 steam car to a 1940s American submarine.

New İstanbul

Across the Golden Horn from 'Old Stamboul' is the 'new' city, often referred to as Beyoğlu, which is actually the name of one of several neighbourhoods that climb the hill from the shores of the Golden Horn and the Bosphorus. There were settlements here long before Christ, and this part of İstanbul is new only in the sense that this was the foreigners' enclave from the arrival of the Genoese in the 14th century. Many of the buildings are in early 20th century Art Nouveau style. Modern high-rise İstanbul is further northeast, in the newer business districts of Maçka and Maslak.

Cross the Golden Horn on the **Galata Bridge**, pausing midway to take in the view. Looking back, Topkapı Palace rises to the left, while the domes and minarets of Hagia Sophia and the

Galata Tower

Blue Mosque fill the middle horizon, and the massive dome on Süleymaniye Camii is to the right. Climbing the hillside ahead of you are the buildings of the new town, with the conical roof of the cylindrical 14th-century Galata Tower rising above them.

Karaköy

Before heading uphill, explore the waterfront district of Karaköy. Once the province of European traders, it is still a port district, with shipping offices, chandlers, and docks that serve Bosphorus ferries and ocean-going cruise-liners. Overlooking the Bosphorus near the mouth of the Golden Horn, **İstanbul Modern** (Tues–Sun 10am–6pm, Thur 10am–8pm; charge/free Thur until 2pm) on Meclis-i-Mebusan Caddesi was originally a customs warehouse on the pier of Karaköy. It now houses a permanent collection of modern Turkish paintings, sculpture, photography, video and sound installations, as well as touring exhibitions, an arthouse cinema and chic first floor café-bar with fabulous views.

Galata Tower to Pera

Back beside the Galata Bridge, board the **Tünel**, a short, steep underground train built by the French in 1875 to link their waterfront offices and hillside residences. At the top, **Tünel Meydani** (Tünel Square) is surrounded by shops and cafés. It is also the southern end of the antique tram line that runs along **İstiklâl Caddesi** to Taksim Square.

At the high point of the hill, **Galata Kulesi** (Galata Tower; observation deck daily 10am–6pm; restaurant offering dinner and cabaret with belly dancers at 8pm; charge) is part of a 14th-century fortifications network built by the Genoese. In the shadow of the tower are several synagogues, some established more than 500 years ago by Sephardic refugees from Spain, invited to the Ottoman Empire by Sultan Beyazit II. The largest one, , has been attacked twice by Islamist terrorists in recent years – in 1986 and again in 2003, with 47 fatalities in total.

Galipdede Caddesi continues up the hillside through an intriguing neighbourhood of narrow alleyways and stepped streets. The **Galata Mevlevîhanesi** (Galata Mevlevî Hall; closed for restoration until 2012) is a former *tekke* (monastery) of the Mevlevî dervish order (see Konya, *page 117*) and now (officially) a museum of calligraphy and dervish memorabilia. When the building re-opens, regular public performances of the order's distinctive whirling, trance-inducing dance, should resume here. Nearby are many shops devoted to the music trade – both recordings and instruments.

Until the early 20th century, İstiklâl Caddesi (Independence Street) was known as the Grande Rue de Pera, and in its smart shops and cafés European residents of the surrounding **Pera** neighbourhood could outfit themselves in Parisian finery, enjoy French pastries and comport themselves as they

Tram on İstiklâl Caddesi

Dracula's head

Just inland from the Galata Bridge, Voyvoda Caddesi is named after the 15th-century prince (*voyvoda*) Vlad III of Wallachia, more familiarly known as Count Dracula. He was a fierce enemy of the Ottoman regime, and after his 1476 death in battle, his severed head was brought to the city from Romania and put on public display.

would at home. Many of the Belle Époque buildings house foreign consulates, originally built as full embassies before the capital was moved to Ankara. Rising above this architectural hodgepodge and adding to the sense of bygone cosmopolitanism are the steeples of Anglican, Dutch Reformed, Franciscan and Greek Orthodox churches.

Nearby, the splendid **Pera Palace Hotel** re-opened in 2010 after a four-year restoration; stop in for a bit of sleuthing, a ride in the birdcage lift and a cup of tea in the Edwardian salon. Built in 1892 to billet passengers travelling on the Orient Express, the hotel has a guest list that includes Mata Hari, numerous royals and statesmen, and Agatha Christie, who wrote *Murder on the Orient Express* here. Her room and the one once occupied by Atatürk have been cordoned off for public viewing. Almost opposite, the equally old Hotel Bristol has come back to life as the **Pera Museum/Pera Müzesi** (Tues–Sat 10am–7pm, Sun noon–6pm; charge), with a fine collection of paintings and Ottoman ceramics, hosting special events as well.

To Taksim

About halfway up İstiklâl Caddesi, a more Turkish atmosphere asserts itself on the alleys and arcades that branch off **Galatasaray Meydanı** (Galatasaray Square). The square is another bastion of European İstanbul, named after the looming edifice that dominates it, a former lycée where Ottoman children were schooled in the French language and Western manners. In the **Çiçek Pasajı** (Flower Market), just off the square, some of the loquacious vendors of the floral displays may tell you that this market is not what it once was – that is, before 1978, when the glass dome and other parts of the structure came crashing down, necessitating a somewhat humdrum renovation. The adjoining **Balık Pazarı** (Fish Market) shows no such signs of modern incursions, and its fishmongers, standing behind voluminous displays of the daily catch as they cajole potential customers, are no small part of the market's appeal. Both markets are lined with cafés and restaurants where in the evening itinerant musicians entertain diners, but you'll get a better, cheaper fish meal along Nevizade Sokak, which separates the two.

The main function of vast **Taksim Meydanı** (Taksim Square), at the northern end of İstiklâl Caddesi, appears to be to accommodate a constant flow of traffic that streams around the Italian-designed **Cumhuriyet Anıtı** (Republic Monument), erected in 1928 to celebrate Atatürk's establishment of a Turkish democracy. The **Atatürk Kültür Merkezi** (Atatürk Cultural Centre; 10am–6pm for tours; evenings for events) is the city's largest concert hall, and has recently re-opened following a two-year renovation.

At the Fish Market

Beşiktaş

Eventually, the royal inhabitants of Topkapı Palace followed the wave of Westernisation and moved across the river to build lavish palaces along the European shore of the Bosphorus. Their mirrored and gilded interiors reflect not prosperity but the 19th-century decline of the Ottoman Empire.

Ⓜ▶   Sultan Abdülmecid sited the **Dolmabahçe Sarayı** (Dolmabahçe Palace; daily except Mon and Thur, Oct–Feb 9am–3pm; Mar–Sept 9am–4pm; guided tours only; charge) in the 17th-century imperial gardens (Dolmabahçe means 'filled-in garden'). The sultan intended the move to symbolize the Ottoman Empire's unveiling the mysteries shrouding Topkapı Palace; Dolmabahçe, however, proved to be a white elephant from the day the soon-bankrupt sultan moved his court here in 1854. Gilded in silver and clad excessively in marble, as per the specifications of the Armenian architects who designed it, the palace is an ornate extravaganza that has long outlasted the crumbling empire it was meant to reinforce. Ironically, the staunch republican Atatürk lived here in the last days of his presidency.

Abdülmecid's brother and successor, Abdülaziz, had far fewer funds to draw upon when, in 1863, he built his own palace on the opposite side of the Bosphorus, the smaller and relatively modest **Beylerbeyi Sarayı** (Tues–Wed and Fri–Sun 9.30am–4pm; charge) and lavished attention on a royal garden, now **Yıldız Park** (daily 9am–6pm), a leafy hillside refuge where his harem was allowed to roam the paths and enjoy the kiosks and pleasure pavilions in relative freedom.

In the 1880s the park became less secluded when Sul-

Stopped clocks

Atatürk died in a simple room in the harem complex of the Dolmabahçe, at 9.05am, on 10 November 1938. All the palace clocks have been stopped to mark that exact time.

Inside the Yildiz Pavillion

tan Abdülhamid II commissioned the 62-room **Yıldız Sarayı** (Tues–Sun 9.30am–5pm; charge) to accommodate visiting foreign dignitaries. The sultan eventually moved in as well. You can still see furnishings he made himself and the tools he used to craft them.

Along the Bosphorus just beyond the Dolmabahçe palace is the **Deniz Müzesi** (Maritime Museum; Fri–Tues 9.30am–5pm; charge). Dry-docked here is an extraordinary fleet that includes imperial caiques and Ottoman war galleys. Other memorabilia ranges from cannons to mementos from Atatürk's yacht.

On the hill above, the **Askeri Müzesi** (Military Museum; Wed–Sun 9am–5pm; charge) tells the story of more than 600 years of Ottoman campaigns and defences. The museum's displays include many *sayebanalari*, elaborately woven tents that sheltered sultans and other royalty on the battlefield, and what is alleged to be fragments of the chain

Martial music

At the Askeri Müzesi, there is a performance of *mehter*, Ottoman martial music, by a Janissary band in full regalia, daily in summer at 3pm. This stirring sound was one of the great influences behind Souza's military marches.

that the last Byzantines stretched across the Golden Horn in a vain attempt to thwart an Ottoman sea attack during the siege of Constantinople in 1453.

Along the Bosphorus

The **Bosphorus** cuts a broad swath through İstanbul, providing a direct artery between the Black Sea and the Sea of Marmara and marking the boundary between Europe and Asia. Millions of ferry-borne commuters criss-cross it each day, dodging under the bows of the supertankers sailing from Russian and Ukrainian ports. It has been a vitally important shipping lane since antiquity and is rich in the city's earliest mythological associations. Jason and his Argonauts allegedly sailed its course en route to and from Colchis. The strait's name comes from Bous (cow) and Poros (crossing place), a reference to an incident in Greek legend in which Zeus turns his lover, Io, into a cow, at which his wife, Hera, spitefully conjures up a gadfly to sting the beast and force her into the stream. Aside from their legendary and historical importance, the straits are also lovely, and a boat trip upstream from the Eminönü docks provides rewarding views of waterside mosques and fortresses, colourful villages, and the distinctive wooden villas known as *yalis*, all backed by forested hills.

Directly opposite Karaköy, Üsküdar and Kadiköy are the main residential suburbs of Asian İstanbul, fairly conservative and traditional in character, with a fine collection of mosques. Offshore, Leander's or the **Maiden's Tower (Kız Kalesi)** is an 18th-century addition to a 12th-century island fortress, used variously as a quarantine centre, lighthouse, maritime tollgate and now, a combination museum-restaurant. Legend has it that a princess was walled up here to protect her from a prophecy that she would die of a snakebite. Perhaps inevitably, the snake wriggled into a basket of fruit and she met her appointed end.

Also in Üsküdar are the **Haydarpaşa Station**, terminus of the Asian railway, and the **Selimiye Barracks**, home of Florence Nightingale's original hospital. From there, it is only a short walk to the moving **British War Cemetery**, final resting place for casualties of the Crimean War and World War I.

Maiden's Tower

Back on the European side of the river, at the western foot of the **Bosphorus Bridge**, is the former fishing village of **Ortaköy (Mesahoro)**, now an enclave of brightly painted wooden houses, a trendy market stalls on the waterfront square and sophisticated cafés or restaurants for well-dressed urbanites. A far less secular sight is elegant **Ortaköy Camii**, these days overshadowed by the lower Bosphorus Bridge, which also shelters the Beylerbey Sarayı *(see page 48)*.

Arnavutköy, the former Greek settlement of Mega Revma, is just upriver. This is a far quieter town, and its atmospheric waterfront is lined with beautifully preserved wooden houses.

Neighbouring **Bebek** is one of the city's wealthiest enclaves, but the presence of the Bosphorus University and an attendant intellectual community lends the town a Bohemian air. The most impressive of the many lavish waterside villas here is the Art Nouveau-style **Hıdıv Sarayı** (Khedive's Palace), which belongs to the Egyptian consulate. The town's famous landmark is the far more imposing fortress of

Who Rules the Waves?

In 1936, the Montreux Convention declared the Bosphorus to be an international waterway because of its strategic importance. The only such waterway bounded by a single country, it is governed by international maritime law, and commercial vessels of any nation enjoy unfettered passage (though there are severe tonnage restrictions on military shipping). In 1936, some 150 ships a year passed through the straits; today it is well over 45,000, thanks in part to the burgeoning Central Asian oilfields. The Turks are nervously expecting a major disaster involving one of the supertankers, and accordingly have strenuously encouraged the construction of overland pipelines to ship Central Asian petroleum.

Rumeli Hisarı (Thur–Tues 9am–4.30pm; charge), massive fortifications assembled by Mehmet II in 1452. Across the channel, completing the pair of sentinels overlooking this narrow stretch of water, rises another early Ottoman castle, **Anadolu Hisarı** (closed to the public).

The next two villages, **Emirgan** on the European side and **Kanlıca** on the Asian side, mirror each other from opposite riverbanks. Each is famous for its local speciality – Emirgan for tulips, which bloom in a hillside park, and Kanlica for sugared yogurt, served in

Boats on the Bosphorus

several waterfront cafés. At Emirgan, the **Sakip Sabancı Museum** (İstinye Caddesi; Tues–Sun 10am–6pm, until 10pm on Wed; charge) is a private art museum. Several rooms have been kept as they were when the Sabancı family lived here, and the collection also includes decorative arts, Ottoman calligraphy and paintings by leading Turkish artists from the 19th century to the present day. The café has live music during Sunday brunch.

At the **Sadberk Hanım Müzesi** in Büyükdere (Thur–Tues 9am–5pm; charge), two waterfront houses contain a magnificent collection of Turkish carpets, tiles and archaeological artefacts amassed by one of Turkey's wealthiest businessmen, the late Vehbi Koç.

when the Sabancı family lived here, and the collection also includes decorative arts, Ottoman calligraphy and paintings by leading Turkish artists from the 19th century to the present day. The café has live music during Sunday brunch.

At the **Sadberk Hanım Müzesi** in Büyükdere (Thur–Tues 9am–5pm; charge), two waterfront houses contain a magnificent collection of Turkish carpets, tiles and archaeological artefacts amassed by one of Turkey's wealthiest businessmen, the late Vehbi Koç.

AROUND İSTANBUL

The Princes' Islands

Only 20km (12 miles) offshore in the Sea of Marmara, the Princes' Islands have been providing a place of escape for centuries, though some notable residents – political dissi-

Phaeton on the carless Büyükada

gardens. Trotsky lived on Çankaya Caddesi in the main town. The most notable structure, topping one of the island's two hills, is the Byzantine monastery of St George. Its three chapels and alleged healing fountain are still pilgrimage sites of great importance to Orthodox Christians.

Heybeli (Halki), the other large island, is less developed, but its terraces of wooden houses are often in better condition than those of Büyükada. The island's Greek Orthodox School of Theology has a famous collection of Byzantine manuscripts, but is not open to the public. Of greatest interest to most visitors are the island's forest paths and lovely, unspoilt beaches. **Burgazada (Antigoni)** has an excellent museum devoted to Turkey's premier short-story writer, Sait Faik (Tues–Fri 10am–noon, 2–5pm, Sat 10am–noon; free). **Kınalıdada (Proti)** is barren and almost completely covered by summer residences (many Armenian-owned), but is said to have the cleanest swimming water of the four islands.

Edirne

In its graceful bridges and other roadside monuments, the Via Egnatia from İstanbul to **Edirne** (today the D100 secondary road) still shows traces of the imperial legions, Byzantines, Ottomans and invading armies who have travelled its length since Roman times. Edirne, 235km (146 miles) northwest of İstanbul on the parallel E80 motorway, lies near the modern Greek border at the heart of the ancient, war-prone region of Thrace. Despite these ancient roots, the city owes most of its outstanding monuments, especially its remarkable mosques, to the Ottomans.

Formerly known as Hadrianopolis after the emperor who made the outpost the capital of Roman Thrace, Edirne fell to the Ottomans in 1361, and served as capital of the growing Ottoman Empire from 1413 to 1458. It was from here that Mehmet II marched on Constantinople. Long after

Edirne lost its role as capital, sultans continued to retreat here to hunt and relax in royal splendour.

The **Selimiye Camii** dominates the city from atop a knoll. This beautiful mosque, completed in 1574, is one of the finest in Turkey, and in building it the great Ottoman architect, Mimar Sinan, set out to surpass Hagia Sophia in majesty. The dome, supported on eight columns set unobtrusively into the walls, creates a stunning celestial effect and, at almost 32m (104ft) in diameter and almost 45m (146ft) high, it is indeed larger than that of Hagia Sophia, if only by a hair's breadth. Inside, exquisite tilework, 999 windows and lacey stonework imbue the massive space with light and serenity. Outside, four

Selimiye Camii in Edirne

identical minarets surround the dome, lifting the entire structure heavenward. The mosque's collection of calligraphy, as well as ceramics and furnishings from throughout Thrace, are on display in the adjoining **Türk-Islâm Eserleri Müzesi** (Museum of Turkish and Islamic Art; Tues–Sun 9am–5pm; charge), originally a medrese (religious school).

You will also see displays devoted to the more earthbound art of *yağlı güreş* (oil wrestling), a popular local sport originally used as part of the soldiers' training. A statue of two wrestlers looms over Hürriyet Meydanı, Edirne's main square. Championship matches are held each summer at Kırkpınar, just outside the city.

The aptly named **Eski Cami** (Old Mosque) predates its more impressive neighbour by almost two centuries and, though its beauty derives mainly from the simplicity of the square plan, its walls are covered in elaborate calligraphy. Surrounding it is evocative evidence of Edirne's importance as a trading centre: the domed, 15th-century *bedesten* (lockable market), the larger Semiz **Ali Paşa Bazaar**, and the **Rüstem Paşa Kervansaray**, which as a hotel conversion continues to house travellers as it has for more than four centuries. A third historic mosque, the 15th-century **Üç Şerefeli Cami** (Mosque of the Three Balconies), just north of the markets, is named for the balconies circling its graceful minarets. Next door the Sokullu Paşa Hamamı, built by Sinan, still functions.

The İkinci **Beyazit Külliyesi** (Beyazit II Complex) lies just north of the city, on an island in the willow-lined River Tunca, reached via the gracefully arched, two-stage **Beyazit Bridge**. Seen from midstream the 15th-century complex, the largest of many such charitable institutions built throughout the Ottoman Empire, is especially remarkable, as hospitals, schools, storehouses and the mosque are clustered beneath a sea of domes. The most evocative of the buildings here may well be the Timarhane, or madhouse, quite enlightened for its time, in which peaceful gardens and splashing fountains were intended to soothe the inmates. It now houses a bizarre little museum of health (daily 9am–6pm; charge).

Oil wrestling

The organised sport of *yağli güreş* (oil wrestling) dates from 1360, when Süleyman Paşa invited 40 champions to wrestle for Allah and the sultan. By dawn next day, the last two were dead of exhaustion, but where each hero had fallen, a spring gushed from the ground. An oil-wrestling festival is held outside Edirne every July; 1,000 wrestlers take part.

İznik

It takes a little imagination to evoke the days when the lake-
side farming town of **İznik**, equidistant from Yalova port and
Bursa, was an important political centre. In AD325, what was
then Nicaea (Nikaia) hosted the First Ecumenical Council of
the early Christian church that proclaimed the Nicene Creed,
establishing the basic tenets of Christian faith still followed
today. In 787, the town hosted another council to resolve the
Iconoclast controversy, decreeing that icons could be worshipped, not as idols, but as conduits to holy personages.

The city briefly became capital of the Byzantine Empire in
the 13th century when the brutal arrival of the Fourth Crusade forced the Lascarid emperors to flee Constantinople. In
1331, it was captured by the Ottoman Orhan Gazi and re-
named İznik. During the next century its craftsmen, many
imported from Persia, began shipping their famous tiles
throughout the Ottoman Empire. Unfortunately, the tiles are
not much in evidence in İznik itself. A few originals are on
display in the **İznik Müzesi** (İznik Museum; Tues–Sun
8am–noon and 1–5pm; charge), alongside ancient coins,
Byzantine jewellery and a bronze statuette of a dancing Pan.
The museum occupies a former *imaret* (hostel) built in 1388
to shelter dervishes and members of the Ahi trade guild.

Across the street, the elegantly proportioned, one-room
Yeşil Cami (Green Mosque) dates from the same period as
the museum and is typical of the Seljuk style. The multi-
coloured tiles that cover the minaret are modern replacements from Kütahya. Also evocative is the **Aya Sofya
Müzesi** (Holy Wisdom Museum; Tues–Sun 8.30am–noon,
1–5pm; charge) in the eponymous church, restored from
dereliction in 2008–09 and retaining damaged floor mosaics
and a faint fresco of Christ, John the Baptist and the Virgin.
Of the four original town gates, at the points of the com-
pass, the most impressive are the easterly **Lefke Kapısı** and

Yeşil Bursa (Green Bursa) and Mount Uludağ

the northerly **İstanbul Kapısı**, both triple-layered affairs built by (or to honour) Emperor Hadrian around the time of his AD123 visit.

Bursa

To see some of Turkey's finest examples of İznik tiles, you need only drive an hour or so west to **Bursa**. This busy, park-spangled city, famous for silk production, peaches, mosques and tombs, sits at the base of 2,543-m (8,342-ft) **Mount Uludağ**, its slopes reached by cable car.

The hillside neighbourhood of **Yeşil**, just above the city centre, is home to two of the city's most famous monuments. The early 15th-century **Yeşil Cami** (Green Mosque) is considered to be one of the great Ottoman masterpieces, and no small part of its beauty derives from the blue and green tiles that adorn its walls to a height of 5m. Especially beautiful tiles decorate the sultan's loge, just above the foyer, and white marble etched with feathery designs covers the elegant entranceway.

The nearby **Yeşil Türbe** (Green Mausoleum; daily 9am–1pm, 2–6pm; free) houses the grandiose sarcophagus of Sultan Mehmet I Celebi and his various offspring. The 19th-century exterior tiles, mediocre post-earthquake replacements of the originals, are in turn being supplanted by new, high-quality İznik work. The interior, however, is awash in a sea of brilliant tilework laid by Tabriz craftsmen during the 1420s.

The Old Centre

The presence of so many monumental Ottoman works in Bursa is a reflection of the city's role in the nascent Ottoman Empire. In about 1312 Osman Gazi laid siege to Byzantine Bursa, which finally fell to his son Orhan in 1326. Orhan proclaimed himself sultan, and the unified empire that began to flourish under his capable stewardship became known as Ottoman, from Osmanli, the clan of Osman. To celebrate his victory, Orhan erected an elegant mosque, the **Orhan Gazi Camii** (much rebuilt since its 1336 foundation).

Living in the Shadows

Each November, Bursa holds a festival celebrating the shadowpuppet theatre that originated here in the 14th century. Local lore has it that Karagöz, a stonemason, and Hacivat, his foreman, broke the tedium of their labours on Orhan Gazi Camii by entertaining their co-workers with humorous, often ribald skits. The pair became such a popular distraction that Sultan Orhan had them beheaded. Regretting his cruelty and missing the pranksters, the sultan arranged to have them immortalised as shadow puppets – Karagöz as a black-eyed, turbaned knave and Hacivat as his hapless cohort.

Among the city's other mosques are two that seem to belong to the realm of the dead. **Emir Sultan Camii**, just east of Yeşil Cami, rises from the midst of graveyards popular with the devout, and the early 15th-century **Muradiye Külliyesi**, comprising a mosque, hamam and , is surrounded by the ten, often ornate tombs of Sultan Murat II and later members of the Ottoman dynasty, many of whom were victims of fratricide, murdered to keep them from interfering with a smooth succession. Nearby, the 19th-century **Hüsnu Züber Evi** (Tues–Sun 10am–noon and 1–5pm; charge) is a restored Ottoman house with a small collection of carved wooden implements made by former owner Hüsnu Züber.

Headstones in the cemetery at the Muradiye Külliyesi

The 20 domes of Bursa's largest mosque, **Ulu Cami**, are allegedly a bargain that Sultan Beyazit I struck when he couldn't fulfil his vow to build 20 mosques if he was victorious at the 1396 Battle of Nikopolis. The fountain beneath the central dome is yet another compromise, made necessary when a local homeowner refused to sell her property to make room for the mosque. The presence of the fountain precludes any possibility of praying on land not donated willingly.

The Ulu Cami is at the edge of Bursa's old commercial district, where the 14th-century covered market *comprises* a confusing warren of little streets where cabinetmakers, cloth merchants and goldsmiths ply their ages-old trades. At the centre of the marketplace is the 1490-vintage **Koza Hanı** (Silk Cocoon Hall), occupied by silk dealers, whose trade – despite decline since the 1700s – is still a vital part of the local economy. In late June and early July, silk breeders fill the courtyard with their little white cocoons, to be auctioned. At other times, the surrounding shops are filled with fabulously sensual silks, from scarves and ties to shirts and richly coloured bolts of cloth.

The elegant suburb of **Çekirge**, 4km (2½ miles) west of the centre, is the best place to stay, with many hotels built on bubbling thermal springs. The Eski Kaplıca and Yeni Kaplıca are both wonderful historic public baths. The heart of the district is the hilltop Birinci Murat Camii, which looks more like a Byzantine church with its brickwork – tradition asserts the builders were all Christian.

THE AEGEAN COAST

Turkey's Aegean coast has been a cultural crossroads for more than 3,000 years. Greeks migrated here early in the 1st millennium BC and founded its marvellous cities. In succeeding centuries, the Persians appeared from the east; Alexander the Great's army marched down from the northwest; the Romans added the area to their empire; Arabs attacked from the south; the Crusaders established military outposts; the Ottoman Empire expanded; and climactic World War I battles were waged. The Aegean coast thus offers the traveller an unparalleled picture of the past – with a backdrop of lovely beaches and old towns, imposing ruins and moving battlefield sites.

Çanakkale

The narrow strait separating Europe from Asia, known in Classical times as the Hellespont and now called the Dardanelles, has proved strategically irresistible to centuries of armies – the Persian Xerxes crossed the strait via a bridge of boats in 480BC, on his unsuccessful campaign to conquer Greece, and Alexander crossed it going the other way 146 years later, on his (successful) march into Asia. In World War I, one of the bloodiest campaigns of this bloodiest of wars was waged just across the strait at Gallipoli.

Çanakkale, a lively navy and university town with a pleasant seafront promenade, makes a good base. The compact old quarter shows traces of a multicultural past in its synagogue, Armenian church, and well-restored bazaar. The **Archaeology Museum** (1.5km/1 mile south of the town centre on the Troy road; daily summer 8am–6.45pm, winter closes 5.30pm; charge) has as highlights of its collection two ornately carved sarcophagi.

Port at Canakkale

Gallipoli

Çanakkale is also a convenient departure point for a visit to the **World War I battlefields** of **Gallipoli**. ◄ 5 Here, in late April 1915, Allied forces launched a massive campaign against Turkish troops to gain control of the Dardanelles and, ultimately, İstanbul. The German commander handed over to his deputy, a young Turkish officer called Mustafa Kemal (later known as Atatürk), who waged a brilliantly ruthless defence of the peninsula. In the months of fighting that followed, more than 46,000 Allied troops and 86,000 Turkish troops were killed and over 140,000 were wounded, out of half of million men on both sides. By January 1916, the Allied troops had retreated in defeat.

Tours to Gallipoli leave from Çanakkale; you can also take the car ferry to Eceabat or Kilitbahir and explore the region on your own. Well-tended cemeteries and other monuments to the dead mark the former battlefields on the peninsula. There's an excellent museum at the Kabatepe

Sea of love

The narrow, dangerously surging waters of the Dardanelles have proved irresistible to romantic swimmers – in ancient times, Leander swam across them by night to visit his lover, Hero, until drowning. The English poet Lord Byron repeated the feat (and surviving) in 1810.

Information Centre, 9km (6 miles) northwest of Eceabat (daily 9am–1pm, 2–6pm; charge), with archival photos, maps, military hardware and touching letters home. Tours tend to visit only the ANZAC and Turkish memorials just north of Kabatepe; if you want to see the English and French sites on the far south cape, you'll need your own transport. The peninsula, incidentally, is ideal for mountain-biking.

Troy

The road to **Troy**, Highway E87, runs 30km (19 miles) south ◀ ⑥ from Çanakkale. The modest ruins of this legendary city lie just west, looking towards the sea (daily 8am–7pm in summer; 8am–5pm in winter; charge).

Homer's famous tale was long believed to be myth, but in 1871 a German businessman named Heinrich Schliemann began excavations at the site and uncovered nine layers of a prosperous city that had stood on the site for at least 4,000 years, including evidence that a battle had taken place at about the time of *The Iliad*. Parts of the massive east wall and gate still stand, a paved chariot ramp leading into the

The Iliad

Homer's story, told in *The Iliad*, is familiar: Paris, son of King Priam of Troy, abducted Helen, wife of Menelaos of Sparta, and took her back to Troy where she was received as his wife. Menelaos immediately appealed to his brother, the great Argive king Agamemnon, and together they amassed an army to get Helen back. For 10 years, the Greeks, including Achilles and Odysseus, tried to conquer the city. Finally, Odysseus hatched a scheme – the Greeks would present the Trojans with a gift of a great wooden horse and pretend to retreat. But the horse was hollow and filled with Greek soldiers; that night, as the Trojans celebrated their victory, the soldiers crept out and opened the gates to the invading Greek army.

city is intact, and trenches and foundations mark the streets and houses of the ancient town. Stand on the ramparts and look over the Troad plain to the sea, where the thousand ships of King Agamemnon laid siege to Troy.

Gold, bronze and silver artefacts, plus jewellery, that Schliemann assembled in 1873 as 'Priam's Treasure' had nothing to do with the Trojan king, as he claimed, but are in fact some 1,200 years earlier in date. They were first spirited away to a museum in Berlin by Schliemann himself, from where they were stolen by the Red Army at the end of World War II. The cache, now the subject of litigation, resurfaced during 1993 in Russia; other objects recovered later are in İstanbul and Ankara. You will need a guide or an archaeological guidebook (available in the site shop) to make sense of the ruins, but it is well worth the effort and will provide an excuse to read one of Western literature's great epics.

Behrarnkale (Assos)

Called Assos in ancient times, **Behramkale** is a divided town: most of its inhabitants live around the imposing ruins, set on a hill, the remainder in the small port below.

7 ▶ **Assos** (daily 8.30am–sunset; charge) may have been a Hittite settlement of the 13th century BC, but its true rise began around 950 BC when settlers from the Greek island of Lesbos just opposite took root here. They constructed a terraced city, much of which remains, on an impregnable site above Aegean shipping routes. In the 4th century BC, Hermias, a former student of Plato, rose to power, instituted a regime based on the Platonic notion of the philosopher-king and founded a school of philosophy, attracting Aristotle, who eventually married the eunuch-king's niece. After Hermias's execution by the Persians, the city passed from one ruling power to the next; the medieval Ottomans dismantled much of the ancient town for building stone.

Assos acropolis, looking up from the surrounding poppies

The view from the ancient **acropolis** is wonderful – down the coast, and over to Lesbos. During the 1980s, inappropriate concrete was used to reconstruct the columns of the 6th-century BC **Temple of Athena**; remedial work is now sourcing stone from the original quarries. Around lie sparse remains of the ancient agora, gymnasium and theatre and the intact, simply proportioned 14th-century **Murad Hüda-vendigar Camii**. The necropolis is well preserved, strewn with pieces of the limestone sarcophagi for which ancient Assos was famous, and about 3km (2 miles) of the old city walls still stand.

The little harbour at the bottom of a steeply twisting road, once used to ship out the acorns from which the region formerly made a living, has a compact collection of restaurants and hotels popular with the İstanbul trendy set. There's no real beach – the closest proper one is at Kadırga, a 45-minute walk (or 4km/2½-miles drive) east.

Ayvalık

Follow the coast road around the Gulf of Edremit to charming **Ayvalık**, 131km (81 miles) south of Behramkale. Founded by Ottoman Greeks in the 16th century, it was a prosperous, ethnically Greek town left all but empty after its inhabitants were ejected from Turkey in 1923. It's been resettled by Muslims from Crete and Mytilini, but its square stone houses and narrow, winding streets overhung with balconies and lined with lovely carved doorways still feel Greek. Stop at the busy central **bazaar** where cobblers and metalsmiths ply their trades. Tall minarets mark the city's mosques, all former Greek Orthodox churches; note especially the **Saatlı Cami** (formerly Agios Ioannis), named after its clocktower.

The best beaches are several kilometres south of the city at **Sarımsaklı**, heavily developed with lines of holiday hotels, bars and restaurants. Boat excursions leave from Ayvalık's

Ayvalık's new harbour

main waterfront every morning. The trip lasts for most of the day and includes the nearby islands such as **Alibey Adası** (**Cunda**), with its miniature, Greek-built version of Ayvalık town, and makes frequent stops for a swim.

Pergamon

Pergamon, 54km (33 miles) south of Ayvalık on Highway E87/550, was once the royal capital of the Attalids, and the most magnificent Hellenistic city in Asia Minor. Give yourself plenty of time here, for this was one of the greatest and most beautiful of all Greek cities, and its ruins speak eloquently of its past.

The city became famous in the 3rd century BC when Lysimakhos, a general in Alexander's army, deposited his considerable treasure behind its walls for safe-keeping before dying in battle in 281 BC. His eunuch-steward, Philetaeros, inherited the lot and set about founding a dynasty, adopting a nephew, Eumenes, to succeed him. Under Eumenes I and his descendants (variously named Attalos and Eumenes), the Attalid rulers of Pergamon defeated the Gauls, allied themselves with Rome, and steadily increased their wealth through war and exploitation of the surrounding silver mines and pasturelands. By the time Attalos III bequeathed the city to the Romans in 133BC, the population was over 100,000 strong, immense by the standards of the day.

The ruins

The ruins are scattered across a large area. Start your visit at the Acropolis, on a rocky hill 6km (4 miles) above modern Bergama, and then explore the Asklepion near the town. Both the Asklepion and Acropolis are open daily 8.30am– 5.30pm in winter, until 6.30pm in summer; separate entrance fees. Limited parking is available outside both archaeological zones, with site maps on sale.

Near the summit of the Acropolis, the Corinthian columns of the 2nd-century AD **Temple of Trajan** have been partially restored. The north stoa once housed Pergamon's famous library, founded by Attalos II. It contained 200,000 volumes, partly written on papyrus and partly on bound parchment, a material the scribes invented when Egypt, fearing that the Pergamon library would outshine the one at Alexandria, banned the export of papyrus. The library was a magnet for scholars and historians until the 4th century AD.

Below is what's left of the Temple of Athena and the Altar of Zeus, the latter excavated by the German Karl Humann during the 1880s. Its magnificent frieze, depicting the battle between gods and titans, now has pride of place in Berlin's Pergamon Museum, along with a collection of other choice portable art from the site.

Ancient ruins at Pergamon

A staircase leads down to the **theatre**, which spectacularly backs onto a vast panoramic valley. Beautifully preserved, its 80 rows of seats could accommodate 10,000 people. Performances took place on a removable wooden stage (you can still see holes for the supporting posts). As in most ancient arenas, the acoustics are superb: a conversationally pitched voice can be heard clearly from the highest seats. Just offstage is the Temple of Dionysos.

Ancient medicine

Classical procedures were systematic, but had striking differences from modern medical practices. The patient would sleep in the temple, after which the physician interpreted the resulting dream and prescribed treatment, be it fasting, sacrifice to the gods or exercise, accordingly. Relaxation and private contemplation were also considered crucial, something we are finally learning again today.

The Asklepion is situated well below the Acropolis. Built in the 2nd century AD under the Romans, it was a centre of ancient medicine. Galen (129–202 AD), perhaps the world's first anatomist and physiologist, trained here before he joined the court of Marcus Aurelius in Rome. Besides a stoa and a theatre, the most impressive remains here are circular temples of Asklepios and Telesphoros.

The town

In the town itself, stop at the **Kızıl Avvlu** (Red Basilica; daily 8.30am–5.30pm, until 7pm in summer; charge). Founded in the 2nd century AD as a temple to three Egyptian deities, it was later converted to a basilica and became one of the Seven Churches of Asia Minor, as referred to in the biblical Books of Revelations. The **Pergamon Arkeoloji Müsezi** (Archaeological Museum; Tues–Sun 8.30am–noon, 1–5.30pm; charge) has those finds from the site not in Berlin.

İzmir and Çeşme

10 Turkey's second city, **İzmir**, 80km (48 miles) south of Bergama on the coast road, is the gritty industrial centre of the region. The city claims to be the birthplace of Homer, but its known history starts with Alexander the Great, who had a dream that inspired his generals to build a fortified settlement here shortly after Alexander's demise. As Smyrna, it prospered under the Romans, suffered under Arab invasions, and enjoyed a long period of prosperity as part of the Byzantine Empire, most notably as a key stop on the Silk Route from Asia. The early 20th century brought disaster. İzmir always had a large Greek, Armenian and Levantine population and, after the defeat of the Ottoman Empire during World War I, the city was occupied by the Greek army in 1919. The large force pressed inland, inciting resistance from the Nationalist Turks under Mustafa Kemal. On 9 September 1922, the victorious Turks entered İzmir after a disorderly Greek retreat; thousands of Armenian and Greek civilians died, and a fire – almost certainly the result of arson – destroyed 70 percent of the city.

İzmir clock tower

The current incarnation of İzmir, with its wide, tree-lined boulevards and characterless buildings, is built on those ruins; only the northerly district of Alsancak, with its ornate Belle

Époque mansions, escaped the blaze. Another survival is the Roman agora (daily 8.30am–noon and 1–5.30pm; charge), just east and inland from the modern **bazaar** (leather is a great buy here). The harbour is best appreciated from the seafront promenade, **Birinci Kordon**, or **Konak Meydanı**, the city's main square with an ornate mosque (1748) and late 19th-century clock tower. Several streets south, in Turgutreis Parkı, stand the city's very good **archaeological and ethnographic museums** (both Tues–Sun 8.30am–5pm; charge).

Just 75km (46 miles) west of İzmir by fast motorway, **Çeşme** is one of the most charming Aegean resorts, crowned by a Genoese castle and flanked by a massive marina. The best local beaches are 9km (6 miles) south at **Altınkum** – scarcely developed white-sand coves. **Dalyan**, 4km (2½ miles) north, is the place to go for quality seafood tavernas. **Ilıca**, east of Dalyan, is a spa-resort with natural hot springs; **Alaçatı**, some 10km (6 miles) east of Çeşme, is a fine old Greek-built town that is the weekend retreat of choice for İzmir trendies, with boutique hotels installed in many of the old mansions.

Sardis (Sart)

Ancient **Sardis** (90km/55 miles east of İzmir on Highway E96/300; daily 8am–5pm, until 6pm summer; charge), lies near the junction of the roads from Ephesus, Smyrna, Pergamon and inner Anatolia – a strategic position that made it, for centuries, the chief city of Asia Minor. Cyrus II (the Great), leader of the Persians, took note of this rich prize, and Croesus, last of the Lydian kings, unsure if

Rich as Croesus

The mountains that surround Sardis are rich in gold ore, and coins were first minted here by the city's last Lydian ruler, King Croesus (560–546 BC), who literally coined the phrase 'rich as Croesus', flaunting his fortune by giving away 10 tons of gold.

he should attack first or wait to be attacked, consulted the oracle at Delphi. The ever-ambiguous oracle replied that if Croesus attacked he would destroy a great empire. Croesus did so, but the empire destroyed was his own. Cyrus used Sardis as the base for his conquest of Asia Minor and his assaults on Greece. Sardis then passed from ruler to ruler over the next centuries until, in AD17, it was destroyed by an earthquake; what remains are ruins of the Roman rebuilding of this fabled city, like Pergamon one of the Seven Churches of Revelations.

The ruins are spread over a large area. The huge **Temple of Artemis**, originally founded by Croesus but rebuilt by Alexander the Great, was never finished; eventually, its stones were looted for use in other buildings. It now consists of a huge foundation with 15 massive Ionic columns, while its setting – amid forested hills and angular rock pinnacles – is very beautiful. About 1300m to the northeast, the **Marble**

Library of Celsus at Ephesus

Court of the 3rd-century AD gymnasium has been beautifully restored. A nearby **synagogue**, also restored, was probably given to the local Jewish community by a Roman emperor in the 2nd century AD; original floor mosaics remain. Entry to this zone is via a marble-paved Roman avenue.

Ephesus mosaic

Ephesus

The gleaming marble monuments of **Ephesus**, 79km (49 miles) south of İzmir on the E87, comprise one of the best-preserved ancient cities on the Mediterranean. The site is open daily from 8am, closing at 5.30pm in winter, 6.30pm in summer; charge. Plan your visit carefully. In high season, arrive early or late to avoid the heat and the tour buses; invest in a site map; and take water. From the car park at the bottom gate, there are taxis or a free shuttle (via a local jewellery store) to the top gate, leaving you an easier walk downhill. Allow time also to visit the adjacent village of Selçuk – the Selçuk museum will illuminate your visit to the ancient city, while Selçuk itself is the site of the great Temple of Artemis, one of the seven wonders of the ancient world.

Set on a sheltered harbour at the mouth of a river, Ephesus was originally built by immigrant Athenians in about 1000BC and dedicated to Artemis. It was conquered by King Croesus, and then held, in relatively peaceful succession, by the Persians, Alexander and the Romans, eventually declining due to its harbour silting up during the Byzantine era. Both St Paul and St John the Evangelist preached here (St John may have been accompanied by the elderly Virgin

Mary), and the city was the site of two church councils. Paul wrote one of his most famous epistles to the Ephesians.

Begin your tour at the uppermost **Magnesian Gate**, from where caravans bound for the east departed in the past. The **Street of Kuretes** heads downhill past the East Gymnasium, Upper Agora and **Odeon**, an intimate theatre for poetry readings and music. The small **Temple of Hadrian** lies farther down the street on your right. Dedicated in the 2nd century AD, this gracious structure, fronted by Corinthian columns, has been restored; the friezes you see are plaster and the originals are in the museum in Selçuk. Behind it are the **Baths of Scholastica**, with their very public communal toilets and beautifully draped, headless statue of the bath's benefactor. Opposite is a large mosaic that presumably fronted a row of shops. Beyond this, steps lead up to the **terrace houses** (daily 8am–5/6pm; charge). These airy, frescoed, mosaic-decorated structures were home to citizens of Ephesus in the Roman imperial and early Byzantine period, and give an idea of what life was like for the well-to-do.

On the corner with the so-called Marble Avenue is the city's **brothel**, marked by a footprint in the stone and some graphic decoration. Rooms surround a central atrium and, in the main reception room, a mosaic depicting the four seasons covers the floor – winter and autumn are the best preserved.

As you turn onto Marble Avenue, the **Library of Celsus**, on your left, is another structure that has been extensively restored by the Austrian excavators. It was erected in the 2nd century AD by the Roman Consul Gaius Julius Aquila, who was subsequently buried in an ornate sarcophagus under the building's western wall. The library housed 12,000 scrolls that were stored in niches separated from the outer walls, to protect them from heat and humidity. Goths destroyed the library in AD262. Beside this, the Lower Agora leads to the incomplete Temple of Serapis.

Back on Marble Avenue, continue to the **theatre**. Started by the Greeks, the structure that stands today is almost entirely Roman – and heavily, if not to say tastelessly, restored. A huge semi-circle backed by Mount Pion, the theatre could seat 24,000. Notice that the pitch increases as you climb up the rows of seats, allowing a clear view of the stage for spectators in the upper reaches. As well as watching plays, viewers over the centuries heard the preaching of St Paul; today, the theatre hosts music and folk-dance performances during the May Ephesus Festival.

The theatre stands at one end of the **Arcadian Way**, the colonnaded main street that runs to the middle harbour gate. Built in the 5th century AD, it was the model of an urban thoroughfare, its shopfronts protected by covered walkways illuminated at night with lamps (only Rome and Antioch shared this distinction). Towards the far end are the massive

The theatre in Ephesus

2nd-century **Harbour Baths and Gymnasium**. To their right, the **Church of the Virgin Mary** was the first church in history so dedicated.

Back on Marble Avenue, turn left to pass the 70,000-seat **stadium** – a venue for everything from chariot races to gladiatorial contests – and the 2nd-century **Gymnasium of Vedius**. A well-preserved monumental gate on the west side was the city's main entrance. The car park, with its ring of overpriced shops and cafés, lies beyond.

Selçuk

Selçuk town began its rise to prominence in the 5th century AD, when the harbour at Ephesus silted up. St John the Evangelist died here in about AD100, and was buried on **Ayasoluk Hill**, which is a good spot to begin your tour. Several hundred years after John's death, the Emperor Justinian constructed an ornate basilica which, until its destruction in the 15th century by the Mongols, was one of the largest in the world. A castle sits atop Ayasoluk Hill; its ramparts provide a fine view. Below it, the **İsa Bey Camii** is an elegant 14th-century mosque.

A quick scramble down the hill brings you to the **archaeological museum** (daily 8.30am–5pm, until 6.30pm in summer; charge). Its wonderful collection of artefacts from Ephesus and other nearby sights includes a bronze statuette of Eros riding a dolphin, a fine wall-painting of Socrates from a reconstructed terrace-house salon, a collection of early crucifixes and various representations of the Virgin and the saints, some fine sarcophagi, and several statues of the many-breasted Artemis, mistress of beasts.

Just out of town, it's hard to imagine how a former wonder of the ancient world could be a less impressive sight than the **Temple of Artemis**, but centuries of neglect and looting have taken their toll. Let your creativity reign, however, and you may be able to re-erect the 127 marble columns, re-create the magnificent friezes and imagine the goddess of the hunt at home and at rest. Another outlying place of interest is **Merye-mana**, the House of the Virgin Mary, on the road from Ephesus to Bülbüldağı. Legend has it that St John and the Virgin lived in this simple dwelling after the death of Christ. Although the story is unsubstantiated, the house has been recognised by the Vatican and is usually thronged with pilgrims.

Kuşadası

Kuşadası, 20km (12 miles) southwest of Selçuk on Route 515, is one of the most popular resorts on the Aegean coast, a port for cruise ships and tour boats and, as such, has become a jumping-off point for group tours to Ephesus. It's a busy place, with some good restaurants and hotels, and the small old centre is atmospheric. To the south of town lies the mountainous **DilekYarımadası Milli Park** (Dilek Peninsula National Park),

The popular resort of Kuşadası

with several good pebble beaches along its north shore. Some 15km (9 miles) north stretches sandy Pamucak beach which, if the wind isn't too strong, also has good swimming.

Pamukkale and Hierapolis

From Kuşadası, Route E87 turns east into Turkey's interior, and the striking scenery and ruins at **Pamukkale** and **Hierapolis** (170km/105 miles inland; daily 8am–6pm in winter, until 7pm in summer; charge).

You will see Pamukkale in the distance as a tall, chalky outcrop rising high above the surrounding plain. Come closer and the rocks will resolve into fantastic shapes resembling flowers, birds, waterfalls. The source of this strange beauty is a spring that, for the past 14,000 years, has burbled up from the top of the plateau, putting out a stream of warm, calcium-rich water that, as it dribbles over the side and cools, precipitates into the hard white chalk called travertine.

The ancient city of Hierapolis may have been founded by Eumenes II of Pergamon. Favoured by the Romans, it became prosperous from trade in wool and an unusual marble coloured by the seepage of minerals. It was also a spa whose waters were

The Antique Pool at Pamukkale

said to cure rheumatism. A large Jewish community laid the foundations for the growth of Christianity, and there were once hundreds of churches here (some of which still stand). The city suffered under Arab attacks, and was virtually abandoned by the 12th century when it passed into Seljuk hands.

While you can hike up from **Pamukkale Köyü**, a vil-

Pamukkale's travertine terraces

lage at the base of the plateau, the main entrance is via a road which winds up the back of the site and through the ruins of Hierapolis. From the top, it is almost irresistible to climb down onto the **travertine terraces**. Pools of milky water are everywhere, but with algae and erosion problems, most areas are closed off with only one walking trail open at any one time. Remove your shoes before stepping in. For a proper bath in the curative waters, visit the once-sacred Antique Pool.

Once cured, step out into the largely Roman ruins. A narrow road leads past the 4th-century AD nymphaeum, or fountainhouse, to the Temple of Apollo. Started in the Hellenistic period and probably completed in the 3rd century AD, it is set on a shelf of natural rock. Not much remains of it. While excavating the temple foundation, Italian archaeologists were troubled by noxious gas seeping from the rock in the Plutonium next door. This sanctuary, dedicated to Pluto, is set over a stream that runs through a deep, natural cutting in the rock. The gas, which includes sulphurous compounds, rises from the water. It is deadly; only eunuchs, according to ancient writers, were immune to its toxicity. Farther along is a restored Roman theatre. Many of the stage buildings have been preserved and, in June, this is the venue for an international song festival. Farther east, past the city walls, is the 5th-century Martyrion of St Philip.

Continue through the triple-arched northerly city gate. The huge arcades on the right were originally Roman baths, which were later converted to a church. Just past them is the ancient city's **necropolis**, dating back to the Hellenistic period, probably the largest cemetery in Asia Minor. For sanitary reasons, burial was not permitted inside the city proper. The tombs, some elaborately designed and inscribed, were surrounded by gardens, and tended by special guilds. Retrace your steps to the baths; a short distance past them is a colonnaded street. Once the commercial centre of the city, it is now traversed by sun-worshipping lizards whose feet scratch lazily over the fallen marble.

The nearby village of **Karakhayıt** has other travertine formations, rainbow-streaked by minerals, as well as a number of hot springs. This is the main tourist centre, with plenty of large spa hotels and a good bazaar. There are two natural mud pools at nearby Karakbaşı and Gölemezli.

Aphrodisias

On the way back to the coast, take Route 585 south through fertile countryside to **Aphrodisias** (80km/50 miles from Pamukkale; daily 8am–5.30pm in winter, until 6.30pm in summer; charge). Named for the Greek goddess of love, the city was a cultural centre, known for its school of sculpture and devotion to Aphrodite. The carefully excavated ruins, built mainly from the local blue-veined marble, give the city an other-worldly air.

Set on a 600-m (1,900-ft) high plateau, and ringed with craggy, marble-veined mountains, Aphrodisias is a strikingly beautiful place. The ruins, most of which date to the 1st and 2nd centuries AD, were obscured by the village of Geyre until 1956, when an earthquake struck. The villagers were relocated a short distance to the west, and excavations have revealed an entire ancient city on a par with Ephesus.

A path loops around the site. The 1st-century **theatre** is beautifully preserved; behind the stage is a large square, or tetrastoön, where Roman and Byzantine citizens might have congregated after a performance. Follow the path anticlockwise from the theatre; below is the **Sebasteion**. This 1st-century complex, consisting of twin porticos and a central paved area, was probably first constructed as a shrine to Aphrodite, and later became a place to honour the Roman emperors. Making an emperor divine and equal to the ancient gods was

Aphrodisias Gateway

a way to legitimise Roman hegemony in the east. A double agora lies just west, its blue-grey marble columns almost indistinguishable from the surrounding poplar trees. Beyond it are the well-preserved **Baths of Hadrian**.

North of the agora, the so-called Bishop's Palace probably began life as the Roman governor's residence. Next are the remains of the **Temple of Aphrodite**. Begun in the 1st century BC, by the 5th century AD the temple had been converted into a Christian basilica and the great statue of the goddess of love that stood here was largely destroyed, her battered torso incorporated into a Byzantine wall. Just north is the school of philosophy, while to the east stands the fully restored Tetrapylon, which marked the intersection of two ancient roads.

Perhaps the finest structure in Aphrodisias is the **stadium**, the best preserved in Anatolia. It was built in the 1st century AD and designed to seat 30,000 spectators. The competitions staged here emulated Delphi's Pythian Games – foot racing, boxing and wrestling; music, oratory and drama. Prizes were modest, and contestants entered simply for the privilege of competition. The **museum** (closed Mon) houses all statuary from the site that hasn't been transferred to major Turkish museums.

Priene

Back on the coast, some 37km (23 miles) from Kuşadası, **Priene** (daily 8.30am–5.30pm, to 6.30pm in summer; charge) is an ancient Ionian city superbly set on pine-clad terraces high on Samsun Dağı. It was probably first settled by Greeks in the 11th century BC. The city whose ruins remain today was laid out in the 4th century BC on a grid system. As the harbour silted up, the wealth of Priene declined, invaders or renovators lost interest, and so it remains an almost purely Hellenistic city.

The ruins are a gentle climb up through the southeast gate from the car park. Main streets run east–west and are intersected by smaller lanes, creating 'insula', which contain either four private houses or the city's public and religious buildings. Note the drainage gutters on the sides of the streets, and the grooves in the centre, which were worn by chariot wheels. Just south of the main street is the 2nd-century BC **bouleuterion**, or council house. Rows of seats on three sides enclose a small stage; a speaker's recess, where speakers stood to address the council, is on the fourth. The building would have been covered by a wooden roof. Across the street are the scanty remains of the sacred stoa, the agora and the Temple of Zeus, which formed the heart of the city. Farther along the main street is a largely residential section of thick-walled houses, their rooms opening off a central courtyard.

On a terrace above the main street stands the **Temple of Athena Polias**. Built in part with contributions from Alexander the Great, it is one of the most harmoniously designed temples on the Aegean coast and served as a model for students of architecture for centuries; five of the original 30 Ionic columns have been re-erected. At the 4th-century BC **theatre**, front-row VIP seating and stage building are largely intact. Finally, if it's not too hot and you are feeling exceptionally energetic, climb to the top of the Acropolis. It will take you more than an hour, but the view is magnificent.

Temple of Athena Polias, Priene

The head of Medusa at Didyma

Miletus and Didyma

Some 14km (9 miles) west, then south of Priene, **Miletus** (Milet; daily 8.30am–5.30pm, until 7pm in summer; charge) is actually the oldest of the ancient Ionian cities. The highlight here is the 2nd-century AD theatre, with seats for 15,000 and fine reliefs on the stage building. Another site standout is the exquisite İlyas Bey Camii, dating from 1404, with a banded dome and finely carved mihrab. Nearby, a museum of local finds is set to open shortly.

Just 36km (22 miles) south of Priene, **Didyma** (Didim; daily 8.30am– 5pm winter, 9am–7.30pm summer; charge) was home to a magnificent **Temple of Apollo** and an oracle, and from its Bronze Age origins was always a sacred precinct, never a town. An early shrine was destroyed by the Persians, and a new temple was planned when Alexander the Great retook the region. Its grand scale almost ensured that it would never be completed and, although work went on for some five centuries, it never was.

Try to visit towards sunset, when the temple's columns glow in the fading light. The temple was designed to be bounded by 108 columns in double rows (some of which have been re-erected), all set on an imposingly high *crepidoma*, or stepped platform. Just below the ticket booth, notice two reliefs of Medusa heads. In a well below the heads, pilgrims would purify themselves, then make their way to the temple shrine, where they would receive the oracle's answers. Further inside the temple is the foundation of the *naiskos*, the great hall that contained the cult statue and sacred spring.

Bodrum

Set on two curved bays, **Bodrum**, 125km (78 miles) from Didyma, is one of Turkey's premier resorts, a rich town that's full of posh yachts, boutiques, restaurants and lively nightlife. The Aegean is never long out of sight, but as the town itself has no beach, many tourist hotels are strung out along the sands of the nearby peninsula.

Known in ancient times as Halikarnassos, the place was colonised by Greeks in the 11th century BC, nurtured Herodotus in the 5th century BC, enjoyed semi-autonomy under the Hecatomnid kings during the Persian era, and declined slowly after Alexander passed through. In the 15th century, the Knights of St John built a castle here; in later centuries the peninsula was home to a largely Greek Orthodox population and, although the Greeks were expelled in 1922, the area retains a vaguely Greek feel.

A view of Bodrum's castle from the harbour

Opening times

The castle is open Tues–Sun 8.30am–5.30pm, until 6.30pm in summer, but the museum halls within it operate a complicated schedule of more limited opening times. Check locally before visiting. There is a separate charge for each hall.

The modern town of Bodrum is dominated by the **Castle of St Peter** on its peninsula, for years the only Christian outpost in Anatolia. Many of the stones in the castle were salvaged from the Mausoleum of Halikarnassos, final resting place of the 4th-century BC Hecatomnid ruler Mausoleus, and one of the seven wonders of the ancient world. St Peter's surrendered to the Ottomans in 1523 and today the castle is a multi-level maze of courtyards, rooms, moats and cisterns. Much of it is given over to the **Museum of Underwater Archaeology**. Don't miss the Glass Wreck Hall, where a Byzantine ship and its cargo, circa 1025, are housed; the Uluburun Wreck Hall, containing one of the world's oldest ships, which sank in the 14th century BC; and the Hall of the Carian Princess, with the lavish contents of a tomb dating to about 360BC. The **towers** offer splendid views across the town and harbour. In the **English Tower** the banqueting hall has been restored, and you can read the graffiti carved in the window niches by homesick knights. Bodrum's bazaar lies just north of the castle. The site of the ancient mausoleum (Tues–Sun 9am–5pm; charge) is two blocks above the harbour; little is left of the mausoleum itself.

A peninsula extends west of Bodrum, with towns and beaches served by both boat and bus. On the south shore, **Kargı** has a fine sand beach and camels to ride, **Karaincir** is another good beach with public access, while **Akyarlar** boasts some good restaurants. In the far west, **Gümüşlük** is a relatively 'alternative' resort with another long beach and the ruins of ancient Myndos. On the north shore, **Türkbükü** fancies itself the St Tropez of Turkey and gets a well-heeled Turkish clientele.

A pretty cove on the Lycian Coast

MEDITERRANEAN COAST

The southern ('Turquoise') coast of Turkey is one of the most beautiful on the Mediterranean, with long sandy beaches, crystal-clear waters and pleasant resorts. This craggy landscape also cradles the evocative ruins of past civilisations, centuries-old cities and spectacular mountain scenery.

Marmaris and the Datça Peninsula

Marmaris is a brash, boisterous resort town and yacht port whose saving grace is a fleet of boats ensuring an easy getaway to more idyllic places. Aside from a seemingly endless line of harbourside drinking establishments, the allure of Marmaris consists of its beautiful setting on a bay framed on both sides by pine-forested slopes and cliffs, and the small, whitewashed old town. An exploration of the narrow lanes begins at the souvenir-filled bazaar and ends at the **castle** (daily 8.30am–

noon, 1–5.30pm; charge), built shortly after a huge Ottoman fleet sailed successfully against nearby Rhodes in 1522. Most of the resort hotels are stretched along İçmeler beach, round the bay to the west, and the closest decent beach.

Datça, 69km (43 miles) west along the eponymous peninsula, proves a workaday market and real-estate town, its town beaches too ordinary to draw may foreign tourists. There's more appeal in **Eski Datça**, 3km (2 miles) inland, a stone-built village that has been restored by Turkish alternative types. From here to the end of the peninsula, the scenery – some of the least spoiled along Turkey's Mediterranean coast – becomes ever more dramatic, with defiles, forested crags, almond orchards. There are the side turnings down to the excellent beaches of **Ova Bükü** and **Palamut Bükü**, both with plenty of accommodation and eating opportunities.

The theatre at Knidos

Palamut Bükü is the last attraction before **Knidos** (daily ◀ **20**
8am–7pm; charge), a 7th-century BC Dorian Greek settlement
draped over a windswept headland commanding the juncture
of the Aegean and the Mediterranean seas. This position on
major shipping lanes earned Knidos a prominent role in the
ancient world. Aside from the rough-hewn beauty of the city's
ruined temples, agora, theatre and Byzantine church, as well
as some curiosities such as the sundial used by the astronomer
Eudoxos, Knidos is more famous for what's no longer here.
The city's famed lion tomb is now in the British Museum, as
is a statue of the goddess Demeter, both unearthed by archaeologists in the 1850s. Most famous in antiquity was the long-
lost, 4th-century BC statue of Aphrodite by Praxiteles. Pliny
praised the sculpted nude as the finest statue in the world, and
travellers sailed here from all over the ancient world to see it.
The road in from Datça is now mostly paved, but you too may
sail in on a boat trip from Datça harbour.

Dalyan

The relaxed resort of **Dalyan** is 75km (46 miles) east of Mar- ◀ **21**
maris, although much closer to the Dalaman airport. The
former agricultural town is lapped by a slow-moving, reed-
lined river, the Dalyan Cayı, beneath a cliff perforated with
4th-century BC Carian rock tombs. Pleasant as these envi-
rons are, a visitor will not be here too long before boarding
a boat and embarking on some extraordinary excursions. A
short way upstream the river opens into **Lake Köyceğiz**, a
former gulf long isolated from the sea, whose reed-beds shelter a rich bird life. Boatmen usually ferry their passengers
upstream first to the **Ilıca mud baths** (40°C) on the river-
bank, and then may continue to the **Sultaniye thermal
springs** (also 40°) on the lake's south shore; the facilities are
a bit basic, but a soak in the warm, mineral-rich waters is
quite soothing.

Loggerhead turtle

Between June and September each year, huge female loggerhead turtles weighing up to 180kg (350lb) drag themselves up onto 17 beaches around Turkey. Each lays around 100 leathery eggs, which take two months to hatch, the babies scurrying in the moonlight down to the relative safety of the surf.

About 1km (½-mile) downstream from Dalyan, boats pull dock below the ruins of the city of **Kaunos** (daily dawn– dusk; charge), famous in antiquity for figs and malaria. Settled in the 9th century BC by the Cari-ans, the city much later passed through Greek and Roman hands and was closely allied with the Lycian civilisation farther east along the coast. This mixed heritage accounts for the presence of Roman baths, a Greek-style theatre, a Byzantine basilica and Lyciantype rock tombs, with elaborate façades suggesting temples. Impressive remnants of the extensive 4th-century BC walls loom just north.

Beyond Kaunos, the river emerges at **İstuzu Beach**. Aside from some makeshift snack bars either end, this flat, sandy beach, 3.5km (2 miles) long, is blessedly devoid of manmade incursions, to protect its status as a breeding ground of the loggerhead turtle *(Caretta caretta)*. You are likely to see the creatures' tracks, but not the turtles themselves, as the beach is off-limits at night during the breeding season.

Fethiye

This busy commercial town, 90km (55 miles) east of Dalyan along Highway 400, is more concerned with the here and now than with the ancient past. Founded in the 5th century BC as Telmessos, it changed hands – and name – several times, to Anastasiopolis and Makri under the Byzantines and finally to Fethiye in the 1930s, in honour of a pioneering Ottoman military pilot.

Earthquakes, the most severe in 1857 and 1957, destroyed the medieval settlement, and most of the ancient one. Just a few temple- or free-standing tombs stand in the streets or are cut into the cliffs bounding Fethiye to the south; the ancient theatre has recently been excavated; a Crusader castle tops the hill behind; and the local museum is replete with local archaeological finds. More compelling, perhaps, are the lively bazaar, and general air of an ordinary Turkish town. Excursion boats depart from here on day-trips to the islands of the Gulf of Fethiye, or multi-day cruises taking in **Gemiler Adası** with its Byzantine ruins, Kalkan and Kekova.

Ölüdeniz and Kaya Köyü

Turkey's most famous beach, **Ölüdeniz**, 12km (7 miles)  **22** south of Fethiye, is much touted on travel posters, the turquoise waters of the lagoon backed by white beaches and

Magnificently situated Ölüdeniz

forested hillsides. The immediate area is a national park; the drawback is that the whole of the valley flanking the approach road is a solid mass of holiday accommodation, and the area is heaving all season, with most arrivals on cheap mass-market package tours that cater to families and young singles. Unspoilt it isn't. To enjoy this lovely coast in quieter surroundings, seek out the beach at **Kıdrak**, 3km (2 miles) east, or take the short boat excursion to '**Butterfly Valley**' and its beach, inaccessible by road.

Kaya Köyü (the medieval Levissi), in a secluded uplands between Fethiye and Ölüdeniz, is a strange ghost town. Its 600 houses and three churches have been abandoned since their Greek Orthodox inhabitants were ousted during the population exchange in 1923. The whole place is now a protected monument (charge when entry booths staffed).

The Ruins of the Lycian Heartland

The tall coastal mountains and fertile valleys east and south of Fethiye and Ölüdeniz cradled the Lycian civilisation. Establishing themselves here even before the Hittite era, the Lycians formed a democratic federation of 23 towns that continued to function even when ultimate

Tlos carpet craftswoman

control was ceded to successive conquerors, including the Persians, Greeks, Alexander, the Rhodians and eventually imperial Rome. The Lycians left behind bountiful traces of their presence, from their coinage to their rock tombs, and a collection of ruined cities that can be reached easily from turn-offs along Highway 400.

Tlos and Pınara

The ruins of Tlos and Pınara crown hilltops on opposite sides of the valley of the Xanthos river, now known as the Eşen Cayı. At **Tlos** (35km/22 miles from Fethiye; open access; charge), the most extensive ruins from the city's lengthy past are its 7th-century BC rock tombs, a Roman theatre juxtaposed against the peaks of the Akdağ range and the Yedi Kapı baths. Relief carvings are unusually rich; one tomb bears depictions of the mythical Bellerophon riding the winged horse Pegasus, while the theatre stage has a block decorated with an eagle and a garlanded youth.

Saklıkent Gorge, the longest and deepest gorge in Turkey

Beyond Tlos, a narrow but paved road leads to the mouth of the **Saklıkent gorge** (dawn to dusk; charge). Some 300m (1,000ft) high and 18km (11 miles) long, this is the longest and deepest gorge in Turkey. Its first 2km (1 mile) is accessible only by a catwalk, then path that follows the base of the towering rock face through icy water pouring out of the limestone mountains of the Gombe Akdağı.

Pınara (across the valley and 20km/12 miles south of Tlos; open access, charge) is less accessible than its neighbour, with final dirt-road approach from the village of Minare. You may well find yourself alone among the ruins scattered among olive trees at the base of a massive cliff honeycombed with tombs.

Intricately carved tombs are also among the best-preserved structures in the town below; the so-called Royal Tomb is decorated with depictions of cityscapes and scenes of what appears to be a religious festival. Across the cultivated plain, the theatre is exquisite – small and perfectly formed, and never modified by the Romans.

The Letoön and Xanthos

The **Letoön** (16km/10 miles south of Pınara; daily 8am–7.30pm in summer, 8.30am–5pm in winter; charge), was a religious sanctuary, a shrine to the goddess Leto and an assembly ground at which Lycians celebrated festivals. The first of the **three temples**, dating to the 3rd century BC, is dedicated to Leto, and French archaeologists have recently re-erected three of its columns, plus most of the walls. The other two temples honour her twin offspring, Artemis and Apollo. A mosaic on the floor of one temple symbolises both twins, with a bow and quiver for Artemis and a lyre for Apollo. The partly waterlogged nymphaeum is well tenanted by noisy frogs; there is also a well-preserved theatre.

Xanthos (directly across the valley from the Letoön; daily 8am–7.30pm in summer, 8.30am–5pm in winter; charge) was the most important of the Lycian cities and its ruins are extensive. The city was noted for its fierce pride and stubborn in-

Lycian culture

Leto was a nymph who had the misfortune of attracting Zeus, thus invoking the wrath of his jealous wife, Hera. Pregnant and in flight from Hera, Leto was befriended by wolves who led her to the Xanthos River to refresh herself. The incident allegedly gave the Lycian culture its name, which derives from the Greek *lykos*, wolf. Leto was not without a vengeful side of her own – she turned some local shepherds who refused her water into frogs.

Ruins at the Letoön

dependence; the residents of Xanthos twice set their city and themselves ablaze in a mass suicide, rather than surrender to the Persian general Harpagos in 540BC or the Roman general Brutus in 42BC.

Like the other Lycian cities, Xanthos is littered with **rock tombs**, including a 5th-century BC pillar tomb with 250 lines describing the exploits of a champion local wrestler; this is the most extensive known script in the Lycian language. The so-called Harpy Tomb is richly carved with figures that are half-woman and half-bird and appear to be ushering the dead into the afterlife. These reliefs are not the originals – they and many other artefacts were carried away from Xanthos in 1842 by archaeologist Charles Fellows. Most, including the Ionic temple known as the Nereid Monument, are now in the British Museum. Among immovable monuments in Xanthos, the city gate and theatre are Roman, the monastery and mosaic-decorated basilica are Byzantine.

Fragments in Patara

Patara

The principal port of Lycia, **Patara** is 18km (11 miles) ◀ 23 south of Xanthos (daily, summer 7.30am–7.30pm, winter 8am–5.30pm; charge). An oracle of Apollo resided here, in a still-unlocated temple; Hannibal and St Paul were among the city's many noted visitors. St Nicholas (who later became identified with Santa Claus) was born in Patara in AD270, the son of a wealthy trader. Today, the ruined ancient city is steadily being excavated, and kept free of the nearby, drifting sand dunes.

The Patara area's other great attraction is a magnificent 15km (9-mile) long blonde-sand **beach**. All development has been kept blessedly far inland at cheerful **Gelemiş** resort, thanks to the ruins and the presence of loggerhead turtles. There is a municipally run snack bar and sunbed concession beyond the beach car park.

Kalkan and Kaş

Relatively free of important ruins, Kalkan and its near neighbour Kaş, both former Greek fishing villages, offer the ruinweary traveller bougainvillea-shaded café terraces, breezy seaside promenades and plenty of retail therapy. Both are charming resorts and excellent bases from which to explore the coast. **Kalkan**, 13km (8 miles) east of the Patara turn-off on Highway 400, is marginally the smaller of the two towns. The old quarter of stone-built, tile-roofed houses, some occupied by shops, restaurants and *pansiyons*, clings to a steep hillside descending to a small harbour. This is, however, completely enveloped by a burgeoning new quarter, most of it second-home developments aimed at foreign purchasers. Kalkan does not a sandy beach, merely a small pebble cove in town and diving platforms on the flanks of the deep bay. Those in need of a real beach make the 6km (4-mile) trip east along the coast to **Kaputaş**, a popular, much photographed beauty spot reached from narrow steps off the roadside and the outflow of an eponymous gorge.

Kaş, a once-sleepy port, 27km (16 miles) east of Kalkan along Highway 400, is now quite lively – especially after dark in high season. However, it retains an easygoing air and a more varied clientele than Kalkan, and the setting, along a curving bay beneath limestone cliffs and olive groves, is lovely. The narrow central streets are lined with small houses and the occasional rock tomb, while a small Greek-style theatre looks out to sea a short walk west from the mosque in the town centre. Kaş is an obligatory port of call for *gulet* trips along the Turquoise Coast, and also the crossing-point to the Greek islet of Kastellórizo just opposite, the remotest of the Dodecanese islands. Both Kaş and Kastellórizo are now official ports of entry/exit for their respective countries, and in season there's at least one daily scheduled ferry in each direction, allowing day-trips.

Old houses in Kaş

Picturesque Kale

Kekova

Kekova Island gives its name to a beautiful and fascinating marine landscape just east of Kaş. You can also drive into the region, following a 20km (12-mile) road off Highway 400 towards the village of **Üçağız** from a turn-off about 18km (11 miles) east of Kaş. Little coastal villages overlook placid inlets, and the seabed beneath the warm waters is divided by the foundations of Roman houses or harbour-works, with Lycian tombs occasionally, and romantically, jutting out of the water.

Üçağız is the larger of the two settlements here, both protected from concrete expansion by existing within archaeological zones, though arrived touristically in a small way. Local fishermen are willing to forsake their lines and nets to ferry passengers to various points of interest. At **Tersane**, the remains of a ruined Byzantine basilica form a picturesque backdrop to a popular spot for swimming from a pebble beach. The north shore of the island is home to the underwater ruins known as **Batık Şehir** (Sunken City), though snorkelling above them is banned to preclude antiquity theft.

The village of **Kale**, reachable by 45-minute walk or another boat ride, huddles beneath a castle built by the crusading Knights of St John atop the acropolis of ancient

Simena. The scramble up the narrow path to the ramparts rewards the visitor with sweeping views and an ancient theatre carved into the living rock inside the castle. Down below, the little harbour is studded with half-submerged Lycian tombs. The incongruous presence of a helicopter landing-pad can be attributed to wealthy Turkish businessman Rahmi Koç, who retreats to a simple house in the village and has endowed several local institutions.

Demre and Myra

Demre, about 35km (21 miles) east of Kaş, is home to the ancient city of Myra and the Byzantine **Church of St Nicholas** (daily summer 9am–7pm, winter 8.30am–5/6pm; charge), built in the 4th century AD during, or just after, St Nicholas's tenure as the local bishop.

The saint's remains were stolen by religious pirates in 1087 and taken to Bari, Italy, but the little basilica still comemorates the saint, whose reputation for generosity seems to have originated from his practice of giving coins to poor households by anonymously dropping them down the chimney. Aside from the *synthronon* (bishops' seating) in the central apse, remains of the original church are difficult to locate among the reconstruction of 1043, and the 1862 renovations that added a belfry and vaulted ceiling over the nave, sponsored by Tsar Nicholas I; Nicholas is the patron saint of Russia, and Russian pilgrims come here in force. Best of the faded Byzantine frescoes are the Communion of the Apostles in the north apse.

Busy saint

As a saint, Nicholas is one of the busiest. Not only is he Santa Claus, but he is also patron saint of Russia, Greece, prisoners, sailors, travellers, unmarried girls, pawnbrokers, merchants and children. The image of the jolly red man with a white beard was a 20th-century invention by the Coca-Cola company.

A short walk or drive north of town brings you to **Myra** (daily 8.30am–7.30pm in summer, 8.30am–5pm in winter; charge). This riverside city was an important centre of Lycian commerce, as evidenced by its impressive monuments – particularly a well-preserved theatre with 35 rows of seats and fine comedy and tragedy masks on the stage masonry. The main group of tombs, some in imiation of wood-beamed Lycian domestic dwellings, are in the palisade west of the theatre; there are more at the so-called River Necropolis, 1500m upstream.

From Demre, Highway 400 follows the indented coastline east for 30km (18 miles) to Finike, from where a 34km (21-mile) steep detour north along Highway 635 brings you to the ruins of **Arykanda** (open access; charge). These cling precipitously to a south-facing hillside to either side of a ravine. Tombs, the agora, a basilica with surviving floor mosaics, a small theatre and a stadium have been excavated. Most im-

Comedy and tragedy masks in Myra

pressive are the main baths, with walls, windows and a plunge-pool still intact.

Olympos and Phaselis

Continuing about 35km (22 miles) east, then north, from Finike, a side road leads to **Olympos**, a long-abandoned port city straddling a tree-shaded stream that disappears into a broad beach just beyond a natural defile guarded by two Byzantine-Genoese forts. The ruins here (daily summer 8am–7pm,

Flame of the Chimaera

winter 9am–5.30pm; charge) are a bit scanty and overgrown, but the setting and opportunity for swimming from the pine-backed beach is memorable. Just before the site entrance is a long series of backpacker-orientated 'treehouse'-style lodges of varying comfort.

Olympos is also the ancient name of the local mountain (one of many summits so called in the ancient world), today called **Tahtalı Dağ** (2366m/7690ft). It's easily visible from **Çıralı**, an alternative base for visiting ancient Olympos, with numerous, more comfortable pansiyons and a separate access road just beyond the first one. Çıralı has two major attractions: a long, scenic beach strictly protected from overdevelopment, with the ruins at one end, and the **Chimaera** (*Yanartaş* in Turkish; open access, but charge), a short way inland from the north end of the beach. Several natural-gas vents here issue eerie flames from the bare rock, as they were doing millennia ago when sailors on Roman trading ships recorded a natural beacon along this part of the coast; they are best viewed at night. It was here that the mythical Bellerophon supposedly defeated the dragon-like fire-breathing Chimaera. There is also an adjacent small shrine to the blacksmith-god Hephaestos, revered wherever fire or lava issued from the earth.

Phaselis (25km/15 miles east of Olympos; daily 8.30am–7pm in summer, 9am–5.30pm in winter; charge) is a former colony of Rhodes and a strategically placed commercial post that traded widely across the Mediterranean, from Egypt to Rome. Phaselitans acquired quite a reputation in antiquity for being both obsequious and venal. The 7th-century BC founders of the city are said to have purchased the territory for some dried fish; their descendants helped both Mausolus of Halikarnassos and Alexander without any prompting, and raised money by selling citizenship for the meagre sum of 100 drachmas. The baths, theatre, aqueduct and wide central street nestle in pine groves around three natural harbours – excursion boats still arrive at the southerly one, and all lend themselves to a swim and a long picnic.

Antalya

Busy **Antalya**, 50km (30 miles) north of Phaselis, was one of the major cities of ancient Pamphylia, founded as a Pergamene colony during the 2nd century BC by Attalos II. While the rest of the coast survives on tomatoes, citrus fruit and tourism, Antalya is Turkey's fastest-growing city, spreading round a broad bay beneath the Beydağları range. The mega-resort hotels are mainly east of town at Lara; however, it's **Kaleici**, the old town surrounding the harbour, that will interest most visitors.

Antalya's most famous landmarks crown the bluffs that surround the harbour. The Seljuk **Saat Kulesi** (clocktower) is built into a fragment of the Roman and Ottoman walls, near the so-called Castle Gate and the entrance to the bazaar. **Mehmet Paşa Camii**, a mosque in front of the clocktower, was built in

Hadrians Gate in Antalya

the 16th century, while a much earlier mosque nearby is most famous for its distinctive **Yivli Minare** (Fluted Minaret); the mosque itself is now a municipal art gallery and the courtyards of its adjoining medrese (theological school) have been glassed over to accommodate shops. Southeast along Atatürk Caddesi, **Hadrian's Gate**, a rather pompous, three-arched monument, honours the emperor's visit to the city in AD130. **Hıdırlık Kulesi**, a contemporaneous stone tower down on the shore, may have served as a lighthouse.

Narrow cobblestone lanes wind down towards the harbour. Many of the Ottoman houses, built in the 19th century and recently restored, now accommodate shops, *pansiyons* and restaurants. Among them is the **Kesık Minare** (Broken Minaret), an eclectic structure that has served as a Roman temple, a Byzantine church and an Ottoman mosque. The downhill walk ends at the old port, a favourite location for an evening promenade.

West of the old town, **Konyaaltı** is the main city beach, its promenade lined by restaurants, cafés, sports facilities and the occasional upmarket hotel. The **Antalya Müzesi** (Tues–Sun summer 9am–7.30pm, winter 8.30am–5pm; charge), at the western edge of the town centre, houses a world-class archaeology collection. Many of the exhibits are from Perge *(see below)* and range from a game board to a pantheon of statuary. Other highlights include mosaics from Xanthos, a silver reliquary that once held the bones of St Nicholas, and Bronze Age burial goods and votive figurines from Elmalı, in the local mountains.

Ruins of the Antalyan Coast

Some of the most extraordinary ancient sites in Turkey make an easy day-trip from Antalya. The neighbouring Pamphylian cities of Perge, Aspendos and Side long predate Antalya, passing through the hands of the Persians and Alexander the Great before becoming a Roman imperial backwater.

Termessos

In a mountainous national park 30km (19 miles) northwest of Antalya, **Termessos** (daily summer 9am–7pm, winter 8.30am–5pm; charge) is one of the most dramatically situated, which allowed it quasi-independence even under the Romans. The city's impregnable position stopped even Alexander the Great, who was deterred by the shower of boulders the citizenry launched from the ramparts above. The climb up to the evocative ruins is still arduous. The theatre's setting – one side abutting a deep gorge and another built into a cliff – is as dramatic as any performance on its stage. A large gymnasium adjoins extensive baths with an elaborate water-collection system, and beyond the odeon and temple complex a hillside is eerily littered with more than 100 tombs.

Perge and Aspendos

East of Antalya, the coast is backed by a broad plain. **Perge**, 15km/8 miles from town along Highway 400 (daily 9am–7pm in summer, until 5pm in winter; admission and parking charges) is not as spectacularly situated as Termessos, but it is unusually well-preserved. Remains of the mundane, including agora shops which still retain their mosaic flooring, and streets rutted by chariot wheels, make it easy to get a sense of everyday life. Monumental Perge is still standing, too, from the red Hellenistic Gate to the huge theatre, baths and stadium, one of the most complete in the ancient world. Continuing east, past the purpose-built golf and beach resort of **Belek**, you come to **Aspendos** (25km/16  miles east of Perge; daily 9am–7pm in summer, 8.30am–5pm in winter; charge). The 15,000-seat **theatre** here, built in the 2nd century AD, is probably the best-preserved Roman the-

The great theatre at Aspendos

atre in the world. The stage, stage building, seats and portico under which spectators gathered in the event of rain are still here, looking much as they did thousands of years ago. The theatre was still in such good repair centuries after its construction that the Seljuks used it as a kervansaray when they occupied the city leaving distinctive zigzag plasterwork over the stage. The theatre continues to host performances during the annual summer Aspendos Opera and Ballet Festival. High above the theatre, on the acropolis, stand a nymphaeum and a basilica; in the distance you can see what remains of an aqueduct.

Timber tryst

It was not the romance of Side's seaside setting that brought Antony and Cleopatra here; rather, the Egyptian queen was trying to strike a deal with Antony for the timber that still carpets the mountainsides to the north of the city.

Side

Side, 22km/14 miles east of Aspendos, is two places: the ruined port evocatively set on a stony headland and a beach resort given over to the worst excesses of package tourism. They are inextricably intertwined – ruins are interspersed with modern souvenir shops, bars and sand dunes, and thus probably more true to Side's past than many other ancient sites. Walking through the monumental gates or looking up the theatre's tiers of 20,000 seats, it is possible to imagine Side ('pomegranate' in ancient Anatolian) as the trysting place of Antony and Cleopatra. It was also the centre of a thriving slave trade. The ruins of the **Temples of Athena and Apollo** are particularly spectacular, poised to catch the sunset at the tip of the peninsula. The **archaeological museum** (Tues–Sun 9am–noon, 1.30–7.30pm, winter 9.30am–noon, 1–5.30pm; charge) stands opposite the theatre.

Alanya

Byzantine church in Alanya

31 Most of the seaside city of **Alanya**, 110km (70 miles) east of Antalya, is relatively new. Though a settlement was already well established here in 44BC, when Antony presented Alanya to Cleopatra, its heyday came later, when Seljuk Sultan Alâeddin Keykubad built his summer residence here in 1221.

The older city crowns a peninsula where Ottoman houses cluster beneath the 7km (4 miles) of walls and 150 towers that surround the castle. Within the enclosure, the inner fortress (daily summer 9am–7.30pm, winer 8.30am–5pm; charge) shelters a ruined Byzantine church with 6th-century frescoes. More popular, though, are the ramparts that afford magnificent sea views – and from which executioners once hurled the condemned to their deaths. Far below, the harbourside **Kızılkule** (Red Tower) now houses the ethnographic museum (Tues–Sun 8am–noon, 1.30–5pm; charge).

Either side of the castle promontory stretch long beaches and the boisterous modern city. The **Alanya Müzesi**

(Alanya Museum; Tues–Sun 8.30am–noon, 1–5.30pm; charge) houses some artefacts from nearby ruins, including a tablet inscribed in Phoenician, kilims and Ottoman furnishings. The nearby **Damlataş Mağarasi** (Cave of Dripping Stones; daily 6am–10am for patients, 10am–7pm for tourists; charge) has elegant stalagmites and is said to be beneficial to asthma-sufferers.

CENTRAL ANATOLIA

A vast, river-slashed plateau, circled by mountains, the Anatolian heartland is relatively little visited but has some of Turkey's most fascinating attractions. These include Çatalhöyük, the world's second-oldest town; Hattuşa, capital of the Hittite Empire; the glorious Byzantine rock churches of Cappadocia; and Ankara, the country's flourishing capital city.

Ankara

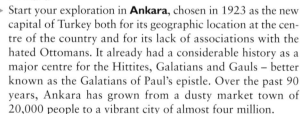

Start your exploration in **Ankara**, chosen in 1923 as the new capital of Turkey both for its geographic location at the centre of the country and for its lack of associations with the hated Ottomans. It already had a considerable history as a major centre for the Hittites, Galatians and Gauls – better known as the Galatians of Paul's epistle. Over the past 90 years, Ankara has grown from a dusty market town of 20,000 people to a vibrant city of almost four million.

Between AD622, when it was taken by the Sassanid Persians, and AD838, when it was sacked by the Arabs, Ankara lived under constant threat from invaders. Its defenders numbered only a fraction of the population of the earlier city and, rather than quarry new stone, they reused material from older buildings to build up the city's defences. The ramparts of **Ankara Kalesi**, mainly dating to the 9th century, are at their most spectacular to the west where a line of triangular towers jut out from the wall. Step through the main gate, and a winding path through little streets – where houses have hardly changed over the past century – takes you left to the innermost point of the castle. Unfortunately, the Ottoman tower is kept locked, but from its base, there is still a fine view. Various old mansions within the walls are now home to restaurants or souvenir shops.

Down the slope to the southwest is the **Anadolu Medeniyetleri Müzesi** (Museum of Anatolian Civilisations; Kadife Sokak; Tues–Sun 9am–5pm; charge). Housed in a former *han* (market with workshops) built by Grand Vizier Mahmut Paşa, this is a truly world-class museum. It showcases the pre-Classical civilisations of Anatolia, from the Palaeolithic, via Neolithic Çatalhöyük, the Assyrian traders of Küllepe and pre-Hittite Alacahöyük, to the Phrygians and Urartians. There are also collections from the Hittite and

The Anıtkabir, the imposing mausoleum of Kemal Atatürk

Late Hittite eras. The contents of the Great Tumulus at Gordion include some very fine Phrygian woodcarvings in astonishingly good condition after 2,700 years. Other things to look out for include Neolithic frescoes from Çatalhöyük, vast Hittite stone sculptures and the exquisite Bronze Age stags found in Alacahöyük.

Across the rail lines in Tandoğan district looms the

Hittite relief in the museum

Anıtkabir, the massively imposing Mausoleum of Kemal Atatürk (Anıt Caddesi; daily 9am–12.30pm and 1.30–5.30pm, with evening sound and light show; charge for museum). The vast tomb hall was built between 1944 and 1953 in a mixture of styles, with stone donated by every province of Turkey. The great man's body, however, is buried in a chamber far below.

Hattuşa, nearly three hours' drive east of Ankara (mostly on the E88) beside the modern village of Boğazkale, was the capital of the Hittite empire from about 1400BC onwards. The site (daily summer 8am–7pm, closes 5pm winter; charge) is distinguished by nearly 6km (4 miles) of perimeter walls, pierced by four surviving gates (including the famous Aslanlıkapı, named after a pair of flanking relief lions). Inside the walls are smaller citadels, and the Büyük Mabet (Great Temple) dedicated to the two main Hittite deities. There was another temple 3km (2 miles) east at **Yazılıkaya** (same hours and ticket); the temple is mostly gone but two ravines flanking its foundations contain fine reliefs of the Hittite pantheon.

Cappadocia

Southeast of Ankara, nature and human ingenuity have together shaped magical **Cappadocia**. Allow yourself plenty ◀ 33 of time – aside from the region's distinctive caves and geological formations, its orchards, fields and forested stream valleys invite unhurried walks, horse rides, or even a hot-air balloon trip. In winter, snow adds a fairy-tale dimension to the already startling landscape.

About 30 million years ago, three nearby volcanoes covered this region in deep layers of ash and mud that solidified into tuff. This soft rock, shaped by the elements into whimsically conical spires called 'fairy chimneys', proved heaven-sent when the inhabitants embraced Christianity – and found that their faith put them at odds with Romans, Arabs and even other Christians. Digging into the pliant tuff, they built secret churches, dwellings, and underground cities that protected up

Cappadocia sentinels

to 20,000 souls from marauders. Even in times of peace, cave dwellings lent themselves ideally to the monastic lifestyle espoused by St Basil (AD330–379), born in nearby Caesarea (Kayseri). Over the years, the ease of digging into the soft tuff has made troglodytes of many Cappadocians. Every village in the region is, at least in part, hacked out of weirdly shaped outcrops.

Ürgüp and Nearby Villages

Transport hub Nevşehir is the largest town in Cappadocia, though **Ürgüp**, tucked into a canyon 23km (14 miles) east, is far more appealing, with its cliffside cave dwellings, cobbled streets lined with handsome Greek-built houses and lively cen-

Üçhisar

tre. Ürgüp is within reach of some remarkable villages. **Mustafapaşa (Sinasos)** is not only near the Göreme Valley and its cave churches, but itself presents an appealing mix of Greek and Seljuk architecture. **Ortahisar** huddles beneath a fantastic, 85-m (240-ft) high rock formation riddled with cave dwellings. At one time this comprised the entire village, and for a small fee you can explore the former dwellings, long since abandoned. **Üçhisar** has also outgrown the tunnelled rock, topped with a fortress (daily summer 7am–8pm; charge), that rises from the village centre, with stunning views over much of Cappadocia.

Göreme

This small town, 7km (4 miles) northwest of Ürgüp, has one big attraction: the **Göreme Açık Hava Müzesi** (Göreme Open-Air Museum; daily 8am–7pm in summer, until 5pm in winter; charge. The former monastic community, dug into cliffs above a verdant valley, was endowed with more than 30 churches from the 9th to the 12th centuries; many of them are decorated with strikingly beautiful, primitive frescoes.

Cave frescoes

The best-preserved cave-church in Cappadocia, the **Karanlık Kilise** (Dark Church), is here with its brilliantly restored frescoes. Most of the other shrines take their names from an object or image contained in their cramped interiors. The Çarıklı Kilise (Sandal Church) is named for the footprints embedded in the floor, said to be those of Christ. The Yılanlı Kilise (Dragon Church) contains a fresco of St George slaying the dragon. Another fresco in this church depicts a full-breasted but hirsute St Onouphrios, a hermit saint of the Egyptian desert. The breasts may reflect an obscure legend in which he was originally a woman, Onouphria, who prayed to god to be made a hermaphrodite in order to not lose her virginity to a persistent suitor.

The Underground Cities

Kaymaklı and **Derinkuyu**, respectively 21 and 29 km (13 and 18 miles) south of Nevşehir (both daily 8am–7pm in summer, until 5pm in winter; charge), are vast underground cities that descend many levels into the earth. They were elaborately equipped with dormitories, sanitation systems, kitchens, wine-pressing facilities, cemeteries and other amenities, all designed to house thousands of refugees for years on end. Comforting as these must have been for those in need of a safe haven, be warned that the narrow passages can induce claustrophobia. Another underground city, **Özkonak** (same hours as above; charge) was discovered as recently as 1972 near **Avanos**; excavations are still underway and visitors can enter only the top four of 10 floors. Avanos, an appealing town on the Kızılırmak ('Red River'), Turkey's longest, has long been renowned for its pottery industry.

Ihlara Valley

The Ihlara Valley

For centuries, this gorge, 100km (60 miles) southwest of Ürgüp, was a lost world. More than 100m (330ft) deep and well off the beaten path, it provided a perfect hideout for early Christians. Over the years, inhabitants dug over 100 churches and monasteries into the cliffs. Reached by steep staircases or paths from the villages of Ihlara, Selime and Belisırma (8am–1hr before sunset; charge), the Ihlara provides excellent hikes along its 16km (10 mile) length and the opportunity to explore the dozen frescoed churches that are open to the public.

Konya

34▶ Konya, amidst endless grain
fields due south of Ankara,
was a Hittite settlement, an
important Roman outpost, a
focus of early Christianity
and a Seljuk capital. It
would then have settled into
relative obscurity were it not
for the Sufi mystic Celaled-
din Rumi – the Mevlâna –
who founded the sect known
as the Mevlevî, or the
Whirling Dervishes. The
Mevlâna Tekkesi (Tues–Sun
9am–5pm, Mon from 10am;

Mevlâna Tekkesi

charge) is among the most important pilgrimage destinations
in the Islamic world, visited by thousands paying homage to
this great teacher.

Rumi was born in Central Asia in 1207 and fled to Konya
when he was 20. Here he met his mentor, a wandering
dervish named Sems-i-Tabriz. Rumi devoted himself to study
with Sems and was inconsolable when his master disap-
peared (possibly murdered by jealous colleagues). Turning
himself to Sufi teachings, he was inspired to write several volumes of spiritual poetry, the *Mathnawi*. Rumi taught his
growing band of disciples to shun ostentation, embrace love
and charity, and elevate the position of women.

Beneath a distinctive blue dome spreads the 15th-century
monastery of the dervishes and the earlier mausoleum of the
Mevlâna. The deceptively humble entranceway lies beyond the
dervishes' tiny monastic cells and the gardens that once sustained the community. Inside, beyond a library where the
dervishes would study, the tomb of Mevlâna rests on a pedestal,

surrounded by the coffins of his eldest son and his father. The adjoining circular hall is the **semahane**, where the *sema (see below)* was originally performed. Reed flutes and other instruments that accompany the dance are on display, as are some rare Seljuk carpets presented to the Melvâna as gifts.

Some 800m west, the **Karatay Medrese** (daily 9am–noon and 1–5pm; charge) is an extensively tiled Seljuk theological school whose dome is decorated with a dramatic representation of the firmaments, once used for astronomical study. A collection of rare tiles and other ceramics are on display in adjoining galleries, grouped around a fountain-cooled courtyard. This medrese and the neighbouring **İnce Minare Medrese** (Seminary of the Slender Minaret; Tues–Sun 8.30am–12.30pm and 1.30–5.30pm; charge) are graced with elegant Seljuk portals ornately tiled in geomet-

Whirling Dervishes

The brotherhood that Rumi founded is best known to outsiders for its distinctive *sema*, a ceremony in which dancers whirl to symbolically free themselves of earthly ties. The position of the arms, with the right arm extending to heaven and the left to the floor, conveys the notion that the dancers are conduits through which the grace of God is flowing to humanity. The dancers' garments also have symbolic significance. The hat represents a tombstone, the cloak is the tomb (and is shed during the dance to represent escape from earthly bonds) and the white skirt is the funeral shroud.

Though the Mevlevî order has been forbidden to practise openly since all religious brotherhoods were banned in 1925, the government has continued to promote the *sema* for its folkloric merit; today, an increasing number of dancers also openly follow the teachings of the Mevlâna, without official interference. Folkloric dervishes perform in Konya during an annual December festival, though you can see more genuine observances at other times in İstanbul *(see page 45)*.

Whirling Dervishes

ric patterns and – a reminder that these were among the first structures built by the nomadic Seljuks – resemble the entrances to tents. The minaret of the İnce Minare Medrese is beautifully tiled but was severely truncated by lightning in 1901; inside is a collection of stone- and woodwork, much of it salvaged from a nearby Seljuk palace. On the knoll between the two medreses, the 13th-century **Alâeddin Camii** has a forest of 42 interior Roman columns, and a finely carved ebony *mimber*.

Çatalhöyük

Çatalhöyük just off the road some 40km (25 miles) southeast of Konya (daily 8am–5pm; charge), is still more of a working archaeological dig than conventional tourist attraction (the best finds are in Ankara), but it has been designated a World Heritage Site by Unesco and is fascinating for students of prehistory. Between about 6250 and 5400BC, Çatalhöyük was a

Early traders

Çatalhöyük contains the earliest evidence in the world of the irrigation of crops and domestication of animals. The people wove textiles, had simple carpets and traded in luxury goods such as black, glass-like obsidian, a rock widely prized for making axes, daggers and mirrors.

prosperous town of some 5,000 people. Rich and poor lived crowded into houses which ran directly onto one another with no streets between them. The only way to gain entry was by climbing through holes in the roofs. Most striking are some wall murals showing hunting scenes and what may be a nearby volcano in eruption.

THE EAST

Eastern Turkey is a hard but immensely rewarding place to travel. The terrain can be challenging and the roads lonely, with long distances between anything; journeys require careful planning. The easiest approach is along the Mediterranean beyond Alanya, with the coast highway passing the enormous Armenian castle (and beach) at **Anamur**, the Hellenistic/Roman town at Uzuncaburç, and a Byzantine double castle at **Kızkalesi** (with another good beach). At Mersin a motorway commences, bypassing dusty Tarsus – hometown to St Paul, and where Cleopatra first met Antony – and Adana en route to the Hatay.

The Hatay and Antakya (Antioch)

A narrow finger of land pointing south towards Syria, the **Hatay** feels more Arabic than Turkish – until 1938 it was indeed part of Syria. This final stretch of the Turkish Mediterranean coast is traditionally Muslim, having little contact with foreign tourists or even sophisticated city-Turks: a fascinating, ancient realm where Hittite and Biblical cultures meet. The regional capital, **Antakya** began life as Antioch in about

300BC, its population soon swelling to nearly half a million. Remains of former glory are few, yet an intense atmosphere seeps through the narrow alleys of the bazaar, making it one of the most charming cities in southeastern Turkey. The **Archaeological Museum** (Gündüz Caddesi 1; Tues–Sun summer 9am–6pm, winter 8.30am–12.30pm and 1.30–5.30pm; charge) is home to a world-class collection of some 50 Roman mosaics. Most of them, carefully removed from Roman villas in nearby Harbiye (the ancient Daphne), date from the 2nd and 3rd centuries AD, and seem to leap off the walls.

During Roman rule, Antioch had a large Jewish community and was crucial in the history of early Christianity. St Peter allegedly lived here from AD47 to 54, frequently joined by the much-travelled Paul of Tarsus and St Barnabas. As a result, Antioch was later the seat of the powerful Patriarchate of Asia, a rival Christian centre to Constantinople –

Roman mosaic in Antakya

chiefly notorious for its heretical scholars. The tiny cave church of **Sen Piyer Kilisesi** (St Peter's Cave), 2km (1 mile) off Kurtuluş Caddesi, northeast of the city centre, is generally regarded as the first Christian church (Tues–Sun 8.30am–12.30pm, 1.30–5.30pm; charge). It was here that the saints first termed their new religion Christianity (Acts 11:26). The fancy façade was built by the Crusaders.

The early church attracted many extremists, including various ascetic monks and other spiritual acrobats like St Simeon Stylites the Younger (AD521–597), who was inspired aged 7 to climb a column on a windy promontory later named **Samandağ** (Simeon's Mountain). He spent the rest of his life on top, fasting and praying, only descending to change to a new column on occasion. The **Aya Simeon Manastırı** (St Simeon's Monastery) grew around his final pillar until an earthquake brought the entire complex into its present state of ruins.

Northern Mesopotamia

Turkey's share of Mesopotamia is of course dominated by the upper reaches of the Euphrates and Tigris rivers, along which the Turks have built a series of giant hydroelectric dams and irrigation canals to turn the neglected barren flatlands into an agricultural powerhouse. A number of remarkable Roman cities and mosaics have been discovered – and drowned – in the process.

The most notable of these is Hellenistic/Roman **Zeugma**, now mostly under the waters of the Birecik dam; fortunately vast extents of mosaic flooring were rescued in time and now form the centrepiece of the **Archeological Museum** (Tues–Sun 8am–noon, 1–6pm; charge) in the booming, one-million-strong city of **Gaziantep**, 35km (22 miles) west. Itself just 100km (62 miles) from Aleppo in Syria, the Arab influence in lifestyle and cuisine – especially in its famous pistachio-based sweets using nuts from the local orchards – is unmistakable. A progressive mayor has seen to the restoration of Gaziantep's remaining old quarters, which once had substantial Christian and Jewish populations.

About 75km (47 miles) south of the **Atatürk Barajı**, now the fourth-largest dam in the world, lies the old town of **40** ➤ **Şanlıurfa**, purportedly the birthplace of Abraham, the father of Judaism. According to local Muslim legend, the cruel Assyrian King Nimrod had Abraham launched from a catapult in the city's citadel, to fall into a pile of burning wood. Happily, God (or Allah) intervened and turned the fire to water and the faggots to fish. Today, visitors

Gaziantep copper craftsman

pray at the **Hızır İbrahim Halilullah complex**, which includes a cave said to be the birthplace of the prophet, and visit a large reservoir full of holy carp.

Some 45km/28 miles south lies **Harran**, with its strange beehive-style mud-built dwellings (now only used as barns), Kurd- and Arab-populated like Şanlıurfa. From here Abraham decided to move into the land of Canaan; under Assyrian rule there was a Temple of Sin, god of the moon, famous for its star readers and savants. Later, Byzantine Emperor Julian the Apostate supposedly worshipped here in AD363 en route to his fatal encounter with Shapur II of Persia farther east. And Harran was a stronghold of the Sabians, planet-worshippers who also used the Sin temple and whose rites only vanished completely long after the arrival of Islam.

41 ▸   The next notable place beyond Şanlıurfa is **Mardin**, spectacularly sited on a castellated crag overlooking the Mesopotamian plain. This small city has an extraordinarily mixed population of Kurds, Arabs, Turks and Syriac Christians, with secular and sacred architecture to match; it has of late become trendy with big-city Turks, for whom a number of high-end hotels and restaurants have opened.

42 ▸   The crowning glory of this region, however, is **Nemrut Dağı** (open access but charge), the only physical legacy of the Commagene kingdom, a tiny state on the upper Euphrates that flourished briefly during the first century BC, managing to stay out of Roman (and Parthian) hands for some time. Built by King Antiochus I Theos (ruled 70–38BC) for his own glory, this fabulous pile of stones and statuary rivals the greatest efforts of the self-deifying, pyramid-building Egyptian pharaohs.

Nemrut Dağı, sacred site of the Commagene dynasty

There is now a road up to the 2,150-m (7,053-ft) summit, and excursions are offered from many of the region's cities (though under your own power it's far more pleasant to stay in the village of Karadut at the base of the mountain). You will be told that you *must* make a visit at sunrise, but this is cold and involves getting up in the small hours; sunset is just as dramatic, and warmer, while mid-day is blissfully uncrowded.

Artificial terraces below Antiochus's presumed burial tumulus are studded with vast statue-heads of Apollo, Tyche, Zeus and Hercules, along with the megalomaniac Antiochus, who included himself in the roll-call of divinities. There are more colossal heads (including two eagles) detached from their bodies on the west terrace, in better condition.

The Far East

Beyond the Mesopotamian plain, the landscape becomes ever more rugged, a high plateau striated by mountain chains under snow eight months of the year, but as before the rewards are commensurate with the trials. From the overwhelmingly Kurdish city of **Diyarbakır**, easily reached from Mardin, it's a straightforward trip to emerald-green **Lake Van**, Turkey's largest at an altitude of 1,650m (5,500ft), with the recently restored Armenian church of **Akdamar** on the **43** eponymous islet. Around Van town itself are more ancient Armenian churches, and the Kurdish-built **Hoşap Kalesi** with a striped bridge below.

North from Van, **Mount Ararat** (Ağrı Dağı; supposedly the last resting place of Noah's Ark), overlooks the engaging pastiche of **İshak Paşa Sarayı** outside the functional town of Doğubeyazit. Next stop for most travellers will be Kars, which bears many marks of its long occupation by Russians and Armenians, and is the natural gateway to **Ani** (daily **44** 7am–sunset; charge), the medieval capital of the Bagratid Armenians, right on the Armenian border.

WHAT TO DO

Exploring classical remains and enjoying the Ottoman Empire's splendours, with some time to relax on a beach, could keep you happily occupied in Turkey. Sooner or later, you will also find yourself immersed in a wealth of other activities.

SHOPPING

Most larger Turkish cities have one at least partially covered bazaar at their centre, and this warren of stalls is still a major shopping precinct despite inroads from modern malls. Any number of small shops usually spill out onto the pavements of the streets surrounding the bazaar. A street market also usually springs up somewhere in town once or twice a week, selling fresh fish, meat and produce alongside ordinary household items.

The most essential tool a visitor can bring to these venues is at least a modicum of skill at bargaining. This age-old art is both an intrinsic part of shopping (except for foodstuffs, which are fixed-price) and a social custom; in fact, it's fair to say that not to engage in at least some negotiating is rude; doing so effectively, however, can take both practice and mettle. See the box on *page 128* for some tips.

Bazaars

In these mainstays of Turkish commerce, a walk down crowded lanes past stalls selling everything from spices to mops is tinged with no small amount of exotic flavour. Bazaars supply household essentials, and those in towns on established travel circuits also cater to visitors with all manner of souvenirs.

Copperware in İstanbul's Grand Bazaar

In İstanbul

The **Mısır Çarşisi** (Egyptian or Spice Bazaar), near Galata Bridge, houses an especially appealing selection of nuts, spices, dried fruits and sweets – as well as nargiles (hubble-bubbles) and every manner of spare parts and compressed tobacco for them – beneath its atmospheric, 17th-century vaulted ceilings *(see page 38)*. The **Kapalı Çarşi** (Covered Bazaar) is perhaps best approached for its colourful atmosphere rather than as a bargain-filled paradise, since tourist-orientated goods tend to be a bit tacky (of the cheap fezzes and lamps shaped like the Blue Mosque variety), and many of the more solid goods offered are ordinary items (including an inordinate number of T-shirts emblazoned with American lingo) geared to locals. Some exceptions include the gold jewellery, antiques and carpets sold in shops near the centre of the bazaar, where you can find dealers of international renown who trade regular-

The Art of Bargaining

While there are no hard-and-fast rules on how to strike a deal with a wily merchant, remember two basics: however clever you think you are, the seller has the advantage of years of experience and will inevitably gain the upper hand (that is, a profit will be made no matter how hard you bargain). It is okay to be casual in the early stages of the negotiation in order to get some idea of price, but the one sure way to infuriate any seller is to engage in hard bargaining when you have no intention of buying. The whole process of buying and selling is charming and entertaining, inevitably accompanied by a glass of çay (tea) and, if you are female, lavish compliments.

It may seem absurd, but whatever price is suggested, come back with an option of roughly a quarter. This gives you both room to wriggle, plead and negotiate until you arrive at a final price that is half or 60 percent of what the seller originally proposed.

ly with New York and London; some silver goods, especially those made and sold in the northeastern corner in what is known as the Kalcılar Han; and the old books and prints in the Old Book Bazaar, near the western gate. The Arasta Bazaar behind the Blue Mosque has some interesting, relatively upmarket souvenir shops.

Elsewhere

Bursa has one of Turkey's most atmospheric bazaars, founded in the 14th century but now housed in a beautifully restored 19th-century structure. This is the place for textiles, with thick cotton

İstanbul's Old Book Bazaar

towels a local speciality, along with silk goods at knockdown prices. Allow time and you can have clothes tailored for you while you visit the local spa. On the resort circuit, both Bodrum and **Marmaris** have large, well-stocked bazaars catering to the many visitors who sail over from the Greek islands of Kos and Rhodes opposite, though the quality of goods in the marketplaces of Fethiye and Kaş is generally superior.

Inland, the *bedesten* (lockable valuables hall) of Kayseri near Cappadocia is now a carpet market, while there's also a covered bazaar devoted to woollens and more carpets. Ankara has a famous copper bazaar, the Samanpazarı, along Salman Sokağı.

Rugs will be laid at your feet

What to Buy

Carpets and Kilims. It would be a shame to leave Turkey without at least one rug, so look forward to the experience, which can be a highlight of your holiday. The crucial point is to do your homework so that you have some idea of prices and quality – and that means being tough enough not to succumb to the first temptation. Walk into any carpet shop and abandon yourself to the dealer. You will be offered a seat and a cup of tea, and the show will begin. Rug after rug will be laid at your feet with a flourish; a savvy dealer will soon detect the size, materials, colours and patterns that seem to be most appealing to you, and eventually bring out only items that match those criteria, narrowing the choices until it seems you must select at least one. Many connoisseurs say the best rugs have long since been brought to İstanbul (which is probably true of the antiques and collectors' items), but you can still find treasures in smaller towns and villages where the carpets are made, or even in highly trafficked resorts such as Bodrum and Antalya.

If you wish to get a feel for quality and price before you start buying, you can ease into carpet-buying by visiting some of the fixed-price, state-run shops or the vast tourist emporia on the coast which have carpet-making on the premises and will show you how they are made and how to check the fabrics, dyes and quality of production, as well as offering potted summaries of the symbolism of the patterns and regional design.

Copper. Ewers, pilaf vessels, teapots, trays, sieves, and samovars handsomely handcrafted from copper were once the mainstay of a bride's dowry, and these items have found their way to many an antiques shop. Besides Ankara, Bergama, Şanlıurfa and Gaziantep are well stocked with au-

Carpet Caveats

A kilim is flat-woven (with no pile) and its pattern is clearly visible on the reverse side. If a kilim is then embroidered, it is called a cicim or sumak. Be wary of claims that dyes are natural. Synthetic dyes have been used for well over a century, and a rug made with natural dyes is likely to be quite rare and expensive. If a dealer insists that a rug is an antique, ask for proof – on the other hand, claims that a rug has been made from old saddlebags or pieces of old kilims may well be true and the result can be uniquely beautiful. If a true antique, you need an export licence.

To ensure colours will not run, rub a wet white cloth over the fabric – if it picks up colour, you know that inexpensive, non-durable dyes have been used. If the material is pure wool, a strand will crumble when lighted; pure silk will turn immediately to fine ash. Smell a rug to see if you can detect the scent of vinegar -- sometimes it is applied to fade colours and 'age' a new rug to add antique value. A reputable dealer will encourage you to perform these tests.

If a rug is hand-woven, the pattern and knots that show on the reverse side will be slightly irregular and the fringe is likely to be uneven as well. The more knots to the inch, the better the quality and the clearer the pattern on the back. Price is according to the amount of work, not the size of the carpet.

A reputable shop will provide a detailed receipt and be willing to ship the rug for you; however, carrying it yourself can reduce the price considerably and also allow you to claim duty-free payments and duty-free allowances. If having it sent, use a reputable international service and ask for a shipping receipt with a tracking number.

thentic copper pieces. Likewise, copper items of modern manufacture – machine-made with a thin sheath of copper over a less expensive alloy – are among the more appealing displays of many bazaars. Some rules of thumb: if it's authentically old, it will be noticeably thick and heavy-gauge, with intricate hand-embossed designs, and expensive; if it's new, it will be quite inexpensive, with any designs likely to be pressed in by machine. Whether old or new, make sure any copper vessel you intend to use is lined with tin (a good merchant will send you to a reliable tinsmith who can do so inexpensively).

Ceramics and tiles. The factories of İznik stopped manufacturing the town's famous tiles on a large scale centuries ago, but since 1993 there's been a modest revival of the craft, and there are now a dozen outlets for practical bathroom or kitchen tiles, trivets, house-number plaques (or just kitsch souvenirs) scattered across the little town. Kütahya, southeast of İznik. is currently Turkey's largest producer of ceramic tiles, and you can find Kütahya tiles, of good quality and in attractive patterns, in shops throughout the country.

The same earth that thrust up the fantastic formations of Cappadocia also yields a bounty of onyx that shows up in bowls, boxes and every other creation; Avanos *(see page 116)* is chock-full of shops selling onyx and pottery made of red clay from the banks of the aptly named Red River, which runs through town.

Clothing. Turkey is one of the world's top manufacturers of fabrics and clothing. You will have no trouble finding imitations of top Western designers – and the genuine article without its label (run-ons from the original order) all over Turkey. For a look at fashionable Turkish couture, step into the shops along and around İstiklâl Caddesi in Istanbul (nearby Rumeli Caddesi and Halâskârgazi Caddesi are especially popular shopping streets); the Galleria in Ataköy on the Asian side is one of several suburban-style malls that outfit the well-to-do with local and foreign fashions. Bodrum and Kaş have some fine small boutiques, while Bursa is famous for silk and cotton manufacture *(see page 59)*.

Leather goods. Turkey produces fine leather, though there are also plenty of poor designer knock-offs and cheap tat. You will encounter tailors offering 'made-to-measure' leatherware in many resorts. Side *(see page 108) and to a lesser extent Alanya* on the Mediterranean coast, seem to have sold their souls to such enterprises, and almost every other shop there now promises to hand-stitch the leather item of your choice within a few hours. Although the workmanship and quality of the leather is often questionable, if you stick to a simple design you will probably walk away with a durable and affordable garment.

Textiles at the Grand Bazaar in İstanbul, Turkey

Array of spices in İstanbul's Egyptian Spice Bazaar

Spices. A popular item in every bazaar, spices often come in handy assortment packets. Beware, however, of seemingly good deals on saffron – the least expensive comes from Turkey, but saffron from Iran is of far superior quality. Pine nuts (especially in Ayvalık or Bursa) can be half the cost of overseas prices.

And keep an eye out for... Blue beads (*nazar*) often worn as pendants to ward off the evil eye; curly-tipped slippers; *nargiles* (hookahs – the best have glass bowls and wood or brass hardware); meerschaum pipes carved from porous stone; inlaid chess sets and backgammon boards, from Syria; fez-style caps fashioned from old kilims; thick cotton bath towels and robes – all of these are easily portable and evocative mementos and are readily available in many bazaars and tourist shops throughout the country. Rather than buy *lokum* (Turkish delight) with its artificial preservatives and colours, keep an eye out for the healthier *cezeriye* (a carrot- and coconut-based sweet).

BATHTIME

Most towns of any size have at least one *hamam* (Turkish bath), as do many larger hotels. Very few offer mixed bathing, with either separate sections or hours for men and women. Prices are generally affordable and some of the finest baths in major cities are historic monuments. Even if they are not, this quintessentially Turkish experience should not be missed.

Upon entering, you undress and wrap yourself in a large, thin cloth (a *peştamal*), which you should wear throughout the ritual (you will be handed a dry towel at the end of the bath). You then enter the sauna-like main chamber, the *hararet*, which is usually domed and tiled. After cleansing yourself in basins at the sides of the room, you will be laid upon the central heated stone platform *(göbek taşı)* and soaped and massaged with a *kese*, a sort of large, exfoliating mitt. Before the final rinse, your masseur will skilfully blow a soapy cloth into a balloon-like ball and give you a refreshing lather. Then relax over a glass of tea or top off the bath with a deep-tissue oil massage (extra cost).

OUTDOOR ACTIVITIES

Ballooning
It's worth getting up at the crack of dawn to see Cappadocia's twisted landscape from the serenity of a hot-air balloon. A memorable, expensive experience is provided by Kapadokya Balloons in Göreme (tel: 384-271 2442; www.kapadokyaballoons.com). Worth every penny.

Birdwatching
As a stop on migratory routes between Europe, Asia and Africa, and with a wide range of terrain, Turkey is rich in birdlife.

Traditional sports

As well as football, which is a national passion, traditional spectator sports include oil wrestling near Edirne *(see page 55)*; winter camel wrestling in the Selçuk area; and *cirit*, a wild and ruthless form of polo.

Among the best places to birdwatch are Kuşcenneti National Park near Bursa; the Çiğli-Sasallı bird sanctuary northwest of İzmir; and the salt lakes and freshwater marshes of Sultan Sazlığı, southeast of Cappadocia, all home (if transiently) to some 250 species.

Golf

You'll find a few links around major cities and resorts. The resort of Belek, east of Antalya, has 11 18-hole courses – some are part of luxury beach hotel complexes. Two courses near İstanbul are Klassis Golf and Country Club (tel: 0212-710 1300; www.klassisgolf.com.tr), and Kemer Golf and Country Club (tel: 0212-239 7010; www.kg-cc.com).

Hiking

There are many fine hiking areas in Turkey, but few well-marked and plotted trails. In the south, there are two – the Lycian Way, which dips and climbs through the mountains along the Mediterranean coast from Ölüdeniz to Antalya; and the St Paul's Trail from Perge to Yalvaç, northeast of Lake Egirdir, with a second branch starting at Aspendos, 40km (25 miles) east of Antalya and joining the first route at the Roman site of Adada. Each takes about a month to complete in total (though many people only do the best bits). English-language guidebooks are available in most Mediterranean resorts. A guide to hiking in the Kaçkar Mountains of northeastern Turkey on existing pastoral paths was published in 2008 by the same team responsible for the Lycian and St Paul's trails. All three areas are covered on the website www.lycianway.com.

Skiing

Turkey has plenty of downhill ski areas, until now mostly appealing to a local audience. Indisputably the best is Panandöken near Erzerum in the northeast; more convenient, if slightly less snowy, are Erciyes Dağı near Cappadocia, and Kartalkaya partway between Ankara and İstanbul. The ski centre on Uludağ near Bursa is the most established, with the most hotels, but is frankly overrated.

Horseriding

Cappadocia is especially well suited to riding, and several local companies hire horses

A horseriding enthusiast

and lead excursions. One of the best is based in Avanos: Akhal Teke (tel 0384-511 5171, www.akhal-tekehorse center.com).

Sailing and Yachting

Many say the only way to explore the Aegean and Mediterranean coasts, with their many coves and inlets, is by boat. Major marinas exist in Çeşme, Kuşadası, Bodrum, Marmaris, Fethiye, Finike and Antalya; tourist offices can give information on facilities and fees *(see page 175)*. Currents and winds along the coasts can be strong; for conditions, tune into shortband waves VHF 16 and 67 for broadcasts in English at 6.30 and 10.30am, and 2.30, 4.30 and 6.30pm.

Many companies offer 'blue cruises' along the coast be-tween Bodrum and Finike in a traditional Turkish craft, a *gulet*. Arrange such cruises either through local operators in most resorts (especially in Bodrum, Fethiye or Marmaris) or through specialists like Cavurali (tel: Turkey, 0242-419 2441; www.cavurali.com), Day Dreams (tel: UK 01884-849200, www.turkishcruises.co.uk), or SCIC (tel: UK 020-8510 9292, www.tussockcruising.com).

Scuba Diving

The abundance of underwater antiquities makes it illegal to dive in certain Turkish waters. There are many authorised areas, however, notably near Bodrum, Ayavalık, Kalkan and Kaş. Dive shops and schools include: Körfez in Ayvalık (tel: 0266-312 4996, www.korfezdiving.com), BT Diving in Kaş (tel: 0242-836 3737, www.bt-turkey.com) and Kalkan Diving (tel: 0242-2361, www.kalkandiving.com). See also www.diveturkey.com and www.scubaturkiye.com.

Swimming

The most enjoyable swimming is from Mediterranean coast beaches; some of the best are at İstuzu, Patara and Ölüdeniz, of which only Ölüdeniz is likely to become crowded, while at Olympos and Phaselis you can swim from beaches backed by ancient ruins. On the Aegean coast, especially nice beach-es and clear waters are near Ayvalık and Çeşme.

Windsurfing and Kite-Surfing

Bitez cove near Bodrum, Fener beach near Akyarlar and the island of Gökçeada (İmroz) are recognised as the three pre-mier windsurfing venues on the Aegean, while at Alaçatı near Çeşme or Gökova near Marmaris you can indulge in kite-surfing. You will find schools and equipment rental available at all these locales.

ENTERTAINMENT

The State Symphony Orchestra, State Opera and State Ballet perform in İstanbul, often at Atatürk Kültür Merkezi on Taksim Square in İstanbul (tel: 0212-251 5600). The city enjoys a cultural flowering from April through July, with the successive International Film Festival, Theatre Festival (even-numbered years), and most famously the International Classical Music Festival, with name overseas acts in historic venues, followed by the Jazz Festival in July; there are other, more traditional jazz events sponsored by Akbank in September–October. For more details, contact İstanbul Foundation for Culture and Arts, Sadi Konuralp Caddesi 5, Şişhane 34433 (tel: 0212-334 0700; www.iksv.org). For other music and arts festivals around the country, *see page 141.*

The **İstanbul State Symphony Orchestra** in concert at the Haghia Irene, İstanbul

Many establishments provide evenings of traditional music and bell-dancing for visitors. In İstanbul, one of the most authentic places to hear Gypsy musicians, with patrons providing their own dancing, is Badehane, at General Yazgan Sok 5, Tünel, Beyoğlu (tel: 0212-249 0550), with live music Wednesday and Thursday. You will find other establishments, often open only in the summer, on your travels up and down the coast and into Cappadocia; tourist offices can lead you to shows in a particular region.

In the resorts on the Aegean and Mediterranean coasts, numerous dance clubs throb late into the night. In central İstanbul the club scene is centred on İstiklâl Caddesi in Beyoğlu, where clubs currently include Babylon at Şehbender Sokağı 3, Asmalımescit (Oct–May; tel: 0212-292 7368, www.babylon-ist.com) and Nardis Jazz Club at Kuledibi Sokağı 14, Galata (tel: 0212-244 6327). In the Bosphorus suburb of Ortaköy, established clubs like Reina (summer only; www.reina.com.tr) and Crystal pulsate.

CHILDREN'S TURKEY

The Turks are extremely child-friendly and the country has plenty of places to engage the young traveller. Much of the history is sufficiently lurid to grab children's attention if presented properly and even if they have had a surfeit of history, ruins are still great places to run and climb. Beaches and boats are superb for family holidays, with plenty of other possible outdoor excursions. Many larger resort hotels have kids' clubs and sports facilities which will take the little darlings off your hands for days on end. Teenagers may well be tempted by the club and bar scene in the resorts, but most clubs are not suitable for the underaged.

Certain foods (kebabs, *pide*, *lahmacun*, salad) suit children well and are healthy. There are occasional problems with food hygiene (especially in summer) and stomach upsets; generally, popular places with high turnover and cooking-to-order are safe. There is plenty of bottled water, but the stuff out of designated town-centre or roadside springs is quite potable (do not drink tap water). It is probably best to avoid the south coast in mid-summer with small children as it can get excruciatingly hot and tender skins can burn easily.

Festivals and Seasonal Events

January Selçuk: Camel Wrestling Festival, 3rd Sunday; also at Denizli, Aydın.

February İzmir: camel wrestling.

March İzmir: European Jazz Days.

April İstanbul: International Film Festival – from Turkey and overseas. Tulip Festival in Emirgan suburb
celebrates a passion for this flower that dates back to Ottoman times.

May Gypsy festival at Edirne, usually 5–6 May; Ephesus: Festival in the ancient theatre; Marmaris: International Yachting Week.

June Aspendos Opera and Ballet Festival; İzmir (Ephesus and Çeşme too): International Music Festival; Artvin: Kafkasör Festival with bulls fighting each other, music, bazaars.

June–July Edirne: Traditional Kırkpinar Wrestling Tournament; İstanbul: İstanbul Classical Music Festival, and Jazz Festival; Çeşme: International Song Contest.

August Ankara: Bilkent International Anatolian Music Festival; Avanos: Tourism & Handicrafts Festival; Hacıbektaş: Hacı Bektaş Veli commemoration, with Bektaşi and Alevî music and dance.

September Bodrum: Ballet & Opera Festival around the castle; Ürgüp: Grape Harvest/Wine Festival with tastings of local wines; Antalya: International Akdeniz Song Contest, featuring the finest voices in Turkey; İstanbul: Akbank Jazz Festival, and Biennial (held in odd-numbered years), the country's top international arts festival, lasting until November.

October Antalya: Altın Portakal Film Festival – increasingly prestigious forum for international and local directors; Bodrum: International Bodrum Cup – yacht race attracting entrants from around the world.

November Marmaris: International Yacht Race – Turkey's last sailing competition of the season; nationwide, 10 November: anniversary of the death of Atatürk.

December Bursa: International Karagöz (Shadow Theatre) Festival; Demre: Special Mass on 6 December honouring Saint Nicholas of Myra, aka Santa Claus; Konya: Mevlâna Festival, 10–17 December – 'folkloric' performances by Whirling Dervishes.

EATING OUT

The pleasures of Turkish cuisine are considerable, and travellers will find it fresh, delicious and varied. Fish caught that day, fresh vegetables and herbs, simply grilled chicken and lamb, and creamy starter-dips are the mainstays of Turkish menus. In fact, a good meal awaits you most anywhere in the country, with the spiciest (some say the best) cooking in the far southeast.

While street food and snacks are available throughout the day in most cities and resorts, you will find a full lunch from noon to 3pm and dinner from 7 to 10pm. Except in the more formal restaurants in large cities, dress is casual.

Even in İstanbul and other large towns, there are fewer full-on restaurants than there are in comparable European cities. Better restaurants, accordingly, tend to be crowded, so you

Döner: the classic Turkish snack

may want to reserve a table in advance; your hotel will probably be happy to do this and arrange for transport as well. Except perhaps in peak season, you shouldn't have a problem finding a seat at resort eateries. During the summer, many resort restaurants stay open well into the wee hours. Many close completely between October and May.

Where to Eat

Especially in İstanbul and other large cities, a wide variety of establishments sell

Cafe Ara on a side street off İstiklal in Taksim

the Turkish version of 'fast food', often at stand-up counters. A *kebapcı* serves the ubiquitous staple of Turkish cuisine, the kebab; lamb is continually being roasted on a revolving spit, ready to be sliced and skewered together with roast vegetables. *Dönercis* offer roast döner, an initially conical mass of fatty lamb or chicken which, as the day goes on ,is whittled down into thin slices served atop bread or rice. A *pideci* offers *pide*, the boat-shaped Turkish pizza, a delicious concoction topped with meats, vegetables, eggs or cheese.

When Turks eat a full meal out, it is usually at a *lokanta*, a simple restaurant that caters to workers at lunch and, often, to neighbourhood families in the evening. The six to eight steam-tray dishes offered at any one time are displayed in a glass case, served on request; most of these establishments offer one or two meat or fish dishes, often prepared as stews, with vegetable and rice or potato accompaniments.

A full-blown *restoran*, or restaurant, is often only marginally fancier than a *lokanta*, but can also be quite elegant. In resorts, restaurant tables spill out onto terraces. Visitors will also find a number of Europeanstyle cafés serving lighter snack meals throughout the day.

What to Eat

Turkish breakfast, available in even the most modest pansiyons, is simple and satisfying. It typically includes sliced cucumber, olives, tomato, a hard-boiled egg, yogurt, seasonal fruit and bread slices to be topped with jam or honey. Only tea or instant coffee is likely to be offered. In multistar hotels, buffet breakfast can be elaborate, with omelettes live-cooked and various charcuterie laid out. Out in town, you can patronise a counter or cart from which *börek*, a fluffy cheese pastry, is served. Later on, the most ubiquitous snack

Grilling fish with lemon

in rural areas is *gözleme*, a crepe-like delicacy stuffed with a variety of fillings.

A full meal at lunch or dinner inevitably begins with *meze*, a wide assortment of delicious hot or cold appetisers (*see pages 147–8 for some of the mezes and other dishes you are likely to find on a typical menu*). Several *meze* platters can in fact be so satisfying that you may not feel the need for a main course.

Main courses rely on various forms of lamb or chick-

Tasty little bites of *baklava*

en; pork is not served in this Muslim country, and when beef makes an appearance it is usually ground. Just about any restaurant, no matter how simple or elaborate, will serve several variations of lamb or chicken kebabs, as well as such staples as *mantı*, a meat-filled ravioli, and *köfte*, meatballs. Fresh fish, often various kinds of bream, is the mainstay of menus along the Aegean and Mediterranean coasts, where restaurants usually display the catch on ice and serve it simply grilled with oil and lemon. In the countryside you are likely to encounter restaurants that raise trout in a pond or stream and serve it at outdoor, tree-shaded tables.

Typical vegetable accompaniments are simply prepared beans, okra or cauliflower, and salad made of tomatoes, onions, peppers, cucumbers, olives and perhaps some white cheese – greens like rocket or lettuce are relatively rare. Popular desserts include *baklava*, phyllo pastry with honey and nuts; *helva*, combinations of flour, butter, sugar and flavourings; or various milk-based puddings.

Turkish wine

Beverages

In this predominantly Muslim country, many restaurants and cafés do not serve alcohol. It's easier to find establishments serving alcoholic beverages – often just beer and wine – in resorts than it is in some of the inland towns less visited by non-Turks.

Turkish wines, mostly made in Cappadocia or along the Aegean coast, are widespread, and many restaurants serve nothing but domestic varieties; the two largest vintners, Doluca and Kavaklıdere, dominate the market, but it's worth asking for local microwinery products. The most popular domestic beers, bottled or draught, are Efes Pilsen, Carlsberg and Tuborg, all at about 5 percent; Efes also makes 'Dark' (6.1 percent alcohol) and 'Xtra' (7.5 percent). By contrast, domestically made spirits like gin and vodka are worth avoiding in favour of imported labels, easily available in most resorts and in more upmarket bars in the larger cities. The alcoholic beverage of local choice, however, is rakı, similar to Greek ouzo and enjoyed before, during and after a meal, mixed with water and ice. The best brands are Efe and Burgaz, though you're likely to be offered only the mediocre Yeni.

Poor-quality instant coffee, irrespective of brand, is almost always referred to as Nescafé; if you want something more satisfying, requestTurkish coffee, usually served *orta şeker-*

li (medium sweet) or *çok şekerli* (very sweet). In major resorts, at least one café will be doing proper, European-style
espressos and cappuccinos – at European prices. Tea, *çay*, is
far more common, and even shopkeepers dispense it freely
to their customers; it is served in small glasses, to which you
can add water and sugar, but never milk, as desired. Bottled
water is easy to find as an alternative to tap water.

TO HELP YOU ORDER...

Do you speak English?	**İnglizce biliyormusunz?**
Waiter!	**Lütfen bakarmısınız!**
What would you recommend?	**Ne tavsiye edersiniz?**

TO HELP YOU READ THE MENU...

Meze (Starters)

antep ezmesi	hot chili purée
cacık	yogurt, cucumber and herb dip
çoban salatası	a salad of tomato, cucumber, peppers, onions and parsley
haydarı	thick garlic dip
imam bayıldı	cold baked aubergines with tomato and onion
mücver	courgette frittata
semizotu	purslane leaves, usually mixed with yogurt
sigara böreği	cheese-filled pastry 'cigarettes'
yaprak dolması	stuffed vine leaves

Et (Meat)

döner kebab	sliced roasted lamb
iskender kebab	döner drenched in yogurt
karısık ızgara	mixed grill
piliç	roast chicken

pirzola	lamb chops
şiş köfte	grilled lamb meatballs

Balık (Fish), Deniz Ürünleri (Seafood)

ahtapod	octopus	karides	prawns
alabalık	trout	kiliç	swordfish
barbunya	red mullet	midye	mussels
hamsi	anchovies	palamut	bonito
kalamar	squid	sardalya	sardines

Sebze (Vegetables)

bakla	broad beans	kuru fasulye	white haricots
bamya	okra	nohut	chickpeas
domates	tomatoes	patates	potatoes
ıspanak	spinach	patlıcan	aubergine

Tatlı (Dessert)

dondurma	Central Asian ice cream
kadayıf	'shredded wheat' filaments in syrup
keşkül	vanilla almond custard
lokum	Turkish delight
aşure	Pulse, wheat, fruit and nut pudding
sütlaç	rice pudding
tavukgöğsü	boiled chicken-breast pudding

Beverages

bira	beer
çay	tea
kahve	coffee
maden suyu	mineral water
arap	wine
ayran	yoghurt drink

PLACES TO EAT

We have used the following symbols to give an idea of the price of a full meal for one, excluding alcohol:

$$$$ over £30 ($50) $$ £10–20 ($16–32)
$$$ £20–30 ($32–50) $ below £10 ($16)

İSTANBUL

Albura Kathisma $$$ *Yeni Akbıyık Cad. 26, Sultanahmet, tel: 0212-518 9710, www.alburakathisma.com.* Everywhere in this district is touristy and pricy, but at least here you get what you pay for and more – excellent service, a pleasant Ottoman architectural environment on several levels, vegetarian options amongst the typical mains, and an unusually full wine list.

Asitane $$$ *Kariye Cami Sok. 6, Edirnekapı, tel: 0212-635 7997, www.asitanerestaurant.com.* Using recipes taken from the Topkapı Palace, the kitchen here prepares spicy, exotic Ottoman dishes that may include – depending on the day and season – lamb with currants, chicken stuffed with nuts and raisins, or spicy, saffron-laced soups. The courtyard is lovely, and classical Turkish music provides just the right touch for a memorable meal. Reservations are advisable as often group events monopolise the place.

Balıkçı Sahabattin $$$ *Seyit Hasan Koyu Sok. 1, Cankurturan, downhill from Sultanahmet, tel: 0212-458 1824, www.balikci sahabattin.com.* Fish specialist working out of a 1927-vintage wooden house in winter, with shaded tables out in the lane during summer; it's not bargain-basement – as the proper table nappery tells you – but the quality is high, with more Turks in attendance than tourists. Fishaphobics should know that there are no meat or strictly vegetarian items on the menu.

Banyan $$$ *Salhane Sok. 3, off Muallim Naci Caddesi, Ortaköy dock, tel: 0212-259 9060, www.banyanrestaurant.com.* A mix of Asian cuisines, from Indian to Thai, at this stylish third-floor eatery with sweeping views of the southerly Bosphorus bridge and the Ortaköy mosque. There's a cheaper fixed menu at lunch, but otherwise expect to pay dearly.

Cezayir $$–$$$ *Hayriye Cad. 12, Galatasaray, tel: 0212-245 9980, www.cezayir-istanbul.com.* Housed in a beautifully renovated and converted 1901-vintage Italian school behind the Galatasaray Lisesi, Cezayir is now one of the most elegant bar-restaurants hereabouts. Several drinking and dining spaces have decor for every taste, while the fare is best described as Med fusion with a Turkish twist; the fixed menus are kinder to wallets. Open 9am–2am daily.

Changa $$$$ *Siraselviler Cad. 47, Taksim, tel: 0212-249 1348, www.changa-istanbul.com.* Kiwi chef Peter Gordon has the beautiful people beating down the doors of his trendy restaurant arrayed over four storeys of an Art Nouveau building, with a glass floor to watch the chefs at work from above and mouthwatering Turkish/Pacific-rim fusion food. Dinner only; closed Sun.

Hacı Abdullah $ *Sakizağacı Cad. 17, Beyoğlu, tel: 0212-293 8561.* Long-established, high-ceiling restaurant serving authentic traditional Turkish dishes. The menu changes regularly, but specialities to look out for include *hünkar beğendi kebap* (beef chunks on aubergine/cheese purée), *kuzu tandır* (roast lamb) and *ayva tatlısı* (stewed quince with clotted cream). No alcohol served. Cash only.

MARMARA REGION AND AEGEAN COAST

AYVALIK

Deniz Kestanesi $$$ *Karantina Sok. 5–9, tel: 0266-312-3262, www.denizkestanesi.com.* The most elegant (and expensive) seafood restaurant in the port district, with a designer interior to match. And yes sea urchin (*deniz kestanesi*) – esteemed like Viagra by Turks – features on the menu, along with local specialities like fried *papalina* (a kind of sprat) and fish roe.

BODRUM

La Jolla Bistro $$$ *Neyzin Tevfik Cad. 174, opposite Karada Marina, tel: 0252-313 7660, www.lajollabodrum.com.* Small, chic bistro whose menu juggles Mediterranean starters, steakhouse standards and sushi, plus Bodrum's largest selection of wines and coffees. Open 9am–11pm daily all year, though sushi bar only in the evening.

Nazik Ana $ *Eski Hükümet Sok 7, tel: 0252-313 1891.* Something of a miracle in often glitzy Bodrum: ultra-cheap, self-serve specials comprising 3 home-style dishes, plus salad. Sweets and beer also available. The stonewalled, canopied courtyard with its wood-bench seating is a cool refuge on a summer day. Cash only.

BURSA

Kebapçı İskender $ *Ünlü Cad. 7A, Heykel district, tel: 0224-221 4615.* One of two local restaurants which claims to have invented Bursa's most famous dish, an artery-clogging pile of *döner* on *pide* slices, slathered in yogurt. That's all they serve. Cash only.

Safran Restaurant $$ *Ortapazar Caddesi, Arka Sok. 4, Hisar district, tel: 0224-224 7216.* Chic, small restaurant attached to the eponymous hotel, with a wide-ranging menu (including meat-mushroom stews and excellent desserts).

ÇANAKKALE

Yalova $$$ *Eski Balıkhane Sok 31, off Yalı Caddesi, tel: 0286-217 1045.* Unusual *mezes* and what's claimed to be the town's widest range of seafood. Dardanelles-view tables upstairs, or in the ground-level conservatory of this historic building, operating as a restaurant under the third generation of management.

ÇEŞME

İmren $$ *İnkilap Cad. 6/A, tel: 0232-712 7620.* The town's oldest surviving restaurant, founded in 1953 by immigrants from

Yugoslavia, has atrium seating and a traditional menu with Balkan touches. The signature dish is *papaz yahnisi* (whole baked carp stuffed with rice). Open all year, daily noon–9pm; cash only.

İZMİR

Deniz $$$ *Atatürk Cad. 188/B (inside İzmir Palas Hotel), tel: 0232-464 4499, www.denizrestaurant.com.tr.* Highly regarded by locals, who return here regularly for speciality seafood dishes like whole fish baked in salt, served in tastefully minimalist surroundings. Good-value set menus; booking advisable. Open all year.

SELÇUK

Ejder $ *Cengiz Topel Cad 9, tel: 0232-892 3296.* A prime location in the pedestrian zone opposite a stork-nested aqueduct, plus a well-balanced menu of meat with an east-Anatolian flair, vegetarian platters and fresh *mezes* combine to make a winner. Cash only.

YAYLAKÖY

Yılmaz'ınYeri $$. *Top of the pass, 9km (5 miles) south of Kuşadası on the road to Söke and Priene, tel: 0256-668 1023.* The best of a cluster of meat-strong restaurants here, always crowded with locals enjoying traditional *meze* in decent portions, an infinity of kebabs, and a very reasonable wine list.

MEDITERRANEAN COAST

ANTALYA

Hasanağa $$ *Mescit Sok 15, Kaleiçi, tel: 0242-242 8105.* Popular, durable old-town restaurant, with a characterful indoor dining area, plus a delightful walled courtyard studded with citrus trees. A serve-yourself buffet *meze* table precedes fish or meat mains. Live Turkish music most evenings. Open all year.

Vanilla $$$ *Hesapçı Sok. 33, tel: 0242-247 6013, www. vanillaantalya.com.* Chic, cozy Turkish-English-run bistro purveying mainly continental fare (steaks, fish, carpaccio, risotto), with Italian/Asian dishes thrown in. First-class service from the owners. Booking advised in season.

DALYAN

Saki $–$$ *Riverbank, by Kral Bahçesi and rowboat ferry to Kaunos, tel: 0252-284 5212.* The only genuine *meyhane* (drinker's tavern) in town, yet family-run, with abundant vegetarian *meze* platters as well as meat mains and (unusually for such an establishment) desserts. Open April–Oct; cash only.

DATÇA

Fevzi'nin Yeri $$ *Behind centre of Kumluk Beach, tel: 0252-712 9746, www.fevzis.com.* Excellent *meyhane*-cum-fish-taverna, with a plethora of old-fashioned *meze* platters rarely seen now, cheerful nautical decor and strictly seafood mains. Cash only.

KALKAN

Kuru'nin Yeri $ *3.5km (2 miles) east of Kalkan, en route Kaputaş beach, tel: 0242-844 3848.* Best of a trio of roadside restaurants clustered here, doling out inexpensive homestyle dishes like *mantı* (ravioli), *nohutlu et* (chickpeas with meat chunks), şakşuka and corn bread. Open all year. Cash only.

KAŞ

Bahçe $$ *Top of Uzun Çarşı, behind Lion Tomb, tel: 0242-836 2370.* The best cold or hot *mezes* in town, served in the garden (*bahçe*). Their seafood annexe just opposite (tel: 0242-836-2779; $$$) is also excellent, with unusual *meze* platters like marinated sea-bass fillet. Both open May to early November.

Sultan Garden $$–$$$ *Hükümet Caddesi, opposite coast guard station, tel: 0242-836 3762.* The place for a romantic tête-a-tête, or a birthday dinner, featuring less common *meze* platters like *paçanga böreği* (turnovers with *pastırma*, tomato, cheese), plus good lamb-based mains. Excellent, genuinely friendly service, and good value for the location. Outdoor terrace open May–Oct, indoor conservatory works winter by demand.

KAYAKÖYU

Cin Bal $ *Signposted in a field, on easterly approach to village, tel: 0252-618 0066.* A locals' favourite, this is a *kendin pişin kendin ye* place, where you buy superb lamb by the kilo and then cook it yourself at a tableside brazier (there's also *tandır kebap* for the lazy). Open all year. Cash only.

PATARA

Golden $–$$ *Central T-junction, Gelemiş resort area tel: 0242-843 5162.* The original (founded 1982) village restaurant here and still one of the best, specialising in trout and grills; almost uniquely in Gelemiş, open all year. Cash only.

CAPPADOCIA AND CENTRAL ANATOLIA

ANKARA

Boyacızâde Konağı $$ *Berrak Sok. 9, Hisar, tel: 0312-310 1515.* Old-house restaurant next to the Museum of Anatolian Civilisations serving on several floors; fairly traditional Turkish cuisine, and splendid views from the outdoor seating.

KONYA

Şifa $ *Mevlâna Cad. 29, tel: 0322-352 0519.* One of the best places to sample the city's version of tandır kebap, baked in a pit until the meat falls off the bones. It's served on pide bread and is finger-licking gorgeous.

MUSTAFAPAŞA (SİNASOS)

Old Greek House (Asmalı Konak) $ *Mustafapaşa (Sinasos), tel: 0384-353 5141.* The restaurant and attached hotel occupy what was the home of the Greek Orthodox mayor before 1923, and the frescoes and original panelling are cared for as lovingly as the home-cooked fare (with lots for vegetarians) is prepared.

ÜRGÜP

Şömine $$ *Cumhuriyet Meydanı, tel: 0384-341 8442.* Local families often join travellers at the long tables on the terrace looking over the town. The hearty food, some of the best in the region, includes stews and house speciality *testi kebap* (spicy lamb with tomatoes, onions and peppers baked in a break-open clay pot).

EASTERN TURKEY

ANTAKYA

Antakya Evi $ *Silahli Kuvvetler Cad. 3, tel: 0326-214 1350.* Owned by a local journalist, this converted 19th-century mansion offers a choice of rooms for dining on spicy eastern Turkish food, including the local *köfte* (meatball) stuffed with cheese, walnuts and olives. It attracts a congenial mix of locals and visitors.

GAZİANTEP

İmam Çağdaş $ *Uzun Çarşı 49 tel: 0342-231 2678, www.imamcagdas.com.* Going since 1887, this is the best restaurant in a city known for its food. The kebabs and *lahmacun* are done to perfection, as is the baklava. Unlicensed. Cash only.

MARDİN

Cercis Murat Konağı $$ *Birinci Cad. 517, tel: 0482-213 6841, www.cercismurat.com.* Founded in 2001 and run by women, this creative restaurant occupies an old Syrian Christian mansion. Regional specialties, often strongly spiced with ginger, cinnamon, coriander, allspice or sumac, include *incasiye* (lamb flavoured with grape molasses, plums and chilis), *kitel raha* (Syrian-style meatballs) and *hmmısiye* (sour chickpea stew). Reservations strongly advised.

A–Z TRAVEL TIPS

A Summary of Practical Information

A

ACCOMMODATION

In general, lodgings fall into two categories: hotels *(oteller)*, found in larger towns and cities, and extending to massive resort complexes along the Aegean or Mediterranean coasts; or guest houses *(pansiyonlar)* which can mean simple, rock-bottom accommodation or, increasingly in the historic quarters of cities and towns, character-filled and comfortable bed-and-breakfast-type lodgings. There is an increasing number of delightfully restored Ottoman mansions opening as small boutique hotels in historic cities at surprisingly affordable rates. All places are officially rated on a scale effectively corresponding to a one-to-five-star system. Technically, the rating reflects the type of amenities offered (pool, restaurant, lifts, etc.) but does not reflect charm or ambience, so a highly desirable establishment can be given a lower rating than a mediocre establishment next door. In some towns, hotels are categorised according to a similar system established by the municipality rather than the national government, and standards can vary considerably from place to place.

Prices are generally considerably less than for similar accommodation in Western Europe and North America, although luxury hotels in İstanbul, İzmir and Ankara charge at international levels. Breakfast – 'traditional' Turkish in simpler places, buffet-style with 'western' options in multi-starred establishments – is usually includ-

I have a reservation.	**Reservasyonim var.**
I'd like a single/double room.	**Tek/çift yataklı bir oda istiyorum.**
With shower	**Duşlu**
What is the price per night?	**Bir gecelik oda ücreti ne kadar?**
Can I see the room?	**Bakabilimiyini?**

ed. Many establishments have single beds only; if you want a double bed, request a *fransiz yatak* ('French' bed), which may or may not be available. Advance reservations are highly advisable at peak season (summer for the entire coast, but also parts of winter in Cappadocia).

AIRPORTS *(havalimani;* see also GETTING THERE)

Most travellers to Istanbul arrive at **Atatürk Airport** (www. ataturkairport.com) 25km (15 miles) southwest of İstanbul. There are excellent transport links, with metro, shuttle buses and taxis to downtown İstanbul (45mins–1hr). The low-cost carriers currently flying into İstanbul, Easyjet (www.easyjet.com) and Pegasus Air (www.flypgs.com), use **Sabiha Gökçen Airport** (www.sgairport.com) at Pendik, about 40km (25 miles) from the centre of İstanbul on the Asian shore. Transport from here is slow, with buses to the city centre (1–2hr depending on traffic); the green E10 bus to Kadiköy connecting directly with ferries (6am–midnight) across the Bosphorus to Eminönü; or taxis which can be very expensive.

There are also a few year-round scheduled services to İzmir and Antalya, plus no-frills flights to these two airports as well as to Bodrum and Dalaman on the Aegean and Mediterranean coasts respectively. Flying into Ankara almost invariably involves a change at İstanbul.

B

BUDGETING FOR YOUR TRIP

Turkey is often inexpensive compared to the euro zone, but prices have risen recently as the currency stabilises and the economy booms. Think of İstanbul, İzmir, Ankara and major resorts as separate entities to the rest of Turkey. In İstanbul or Bodrum, for example, you can get a good double room for US$100–$150/£60–93; elsewhere, you can usually find one for half that amount.

Meals along the coast, and in İstanbul, tend to cost what they do in most of the European Mediterranean; inland prices drop sharply.

Generally, two people can eat extremely well for about $50/£30 and have a pleasant, simple meal for about $35/£22 (with beer, not wine) and a light snack for under $20/£13. Seafood is considerably more expensive than meat, beer is on the cheap side, but wine and *rakı* are relatively dear. Coffee is more expensive than tea, especially if it's cappuccino or espresso. Petrol is about the most expensive in the world, yet local transport remains affordable; on-line specials for domestic air tickets can often nearly match bus fares.

C

CAMPING *(kamping)*

Camping is practised at relatively few designated sites (mostly along the Aegean and Mediterranean coasts) and along long distance trails such as the Lycian Way or St Paul Trail. The most pleasant sites, especially if you have a caravan or camper van, are the 20 or so run by the Ministry of Forestry – look for yellow lettering on brown wooden signs.

CAR HIRE

To hire a car, you must be over 21 and have had a licence for a year. You will also need a credit card for the damages deposit. The major companies all have outlets in Turkey and there are also many local hire-car agencies. Antalya, Bodrum, Dalaman airport and (sometimes) İzmir airport are the least expensive places to pick up a car; İstanbul, Marmaris, Kuşadası, Çeşme and anywhere in the east are the most expensive. Booking on-line will often be much cheaper, especially for longer periods. If you have an accident when driving a hire car in Turkey, notify the police immediately; insurance claims are invalid unless accompanied by an official accident report (*kaza raporu*).

CLIMATE

Turkey is given to great extremes of climate. Expect high summer temperatures everywhere, cold, damp winters in İstanbul and Cappadocia (where, as elsewhere in Central Anatolia, it can be bitterly cold and snowy), and mild winters on the Mediterranean and Aegean coasts. Especially pleasant times to visit Turkey are spring and autumn, when temperatures are moderate and crowds are thin.

Istanbul:	J	F	M	A	M	J	J	A	S	O	N	D
°C max	8	9	11	16	21	25	28	28	24	20	15	11
°C min	3	2	3	7	12	16	18	19	16	13	9	5
	J	F	M	A	M	J	J	A	S	O	N	D
°F max	46	47	51	60	69	77	82	82	76	68	59	51
°F min	37	36	38	45	53	60	65	66	61	55	48	41

Ankara:	J	F	M	A	M	J	J	A	S	O	N	D
°C max	4	6	11	17	23	26	30	31	26	21	14	6
°C min	-4	-3	-1	4	9	12	15	15	11	7	3	-2
	J	F	M	A	M	J	J	A	S	O	N	D
°F max	39	42	51	63	73	78	86	87	78	69	57	43
°F min	24	26	31	40	49	53	59	59	52	44	37	29

İzmir:	J	F	M	A	M	J	J	A	S	O	N	D
°C max	13	14	17	21	26	31	33	33	29	24	19	14
°C min	4	4	6	9	13	17	21	21	17	13	9	6
	J	F	M	A	M	J	J	A	S	O	N	D
°F max	55	57	63	70	79	87	92	92	85	76	67	58
°F min	39	40	43	49	56	63	69	69	62	55	49	42

Antalya:	J	F	M	A	M	J	J	A	S	O	N	D
°C max	15	16	18	21	26	30	34	33	31	27	22	17
°C min	6	7	8	11	16	19	23	22	19	15	11	8
	J	F	M	A	M	J	J	A	S	O	N	D
°F max	59	61	65	70	79	86	94	92	88	81	72	63
°F min	43	45	47	52	61	67	74	72	67	59	52	47

CLOTHING

Although Turks have become inured to the sight of tourists clad in shorts and T-shirts tramping through their cities, they do not like the practice. This is an Islamic country and while they do not expect you to wear the veil, keeping your shoulders and knees covered away from the beach is only polite. It's a necessity if you are planning to visit any mosques (where women may also be expected to cover their heads and both sexes are required to remove their shoes). The general summer dress is lightweight trousers and short-sleeved button-down or polo shirts for men, and trousers and blouses, skirts, or dresses for women. Bathing suits, vests, brief shorts and other skimpy attire are not to be worn anywhere other than the beach. When visiting archaeological sites, you'll want sturdy walking or hiking shoes for scrambles up rough paths. A hat and sunglasses are necessities in summer and sensible at most times.

From October through to April you will need a pullover or two in the south; in the centre and north, including İstanbul, you may need full-blown winter gear as temperatures fall, rain is common and it will usually snow at some point.

Only the most expensive restaurants in İstanbul require jacket-and-tie formality, but you will want to dress well, even if casually so, for dinner in better restaurants anywhere in the country.

CRIME AND SAFETY

Turkey is relatively safe, and even in İstanbul crime is rarely more serious than pick-pocketing or purse-snatching; be especially careful in crowded markets and in metro cars. This said, you should be aware of some scams that are periodically perpetrated against tourists. One involves İstanbul cab drivers taking your money, substituting it with lower-denomination bills, and flashing them at you insisting that you have underpaid; to avoid this situation, tally the money you are handing the driver and call for the police immediately if an argument ensues. Far more serious is someone (usually a man) who will offer assistance with directions, only to lure you to an accomplice who may attempt to mug you.

Two of the most serious offences tourists might commit are possession of illicit drugs or antiquities; both incursions are punishable by stiff prison sentences and are not to be taken lightly.

D

DRIVING

Turkey's roads are not for the faint of heart and you need to drive defensively at all times. While some major highways, including the country's growing number of toll motorways, are well designed and well maintained, many roads are poorly paved, poorly marked and lit, erratically signposted and dangerously curvy and narrow, with relatively few crash barriers on cliff roads. The Turks tend to drive fast and often recklessly – expect sudden stops, heedless pulling out of side roads, turns without signals, overtaking on all sides. In rural areas, you are quite likely to come upon flocks of sheep and goats in the road, as well as elderly and overloaded trucks, children playing football or donkey carts headed down the carriageway in the wrong direction. All of these pose an extra hazard at night, especially with the frequent presence of unlit vehicles. Traffic lights go straight from red to green; a flashing yellow arrow means you can turn right if the road is clear even if the main light is red.

You may drive on your national driver's licence for up to three months, but an IDP is most useful for flashing at the many control points. If bringing a car into Turkey, you will need the logbook, proof of ownership, a Green Card and carnet. Check you are comprehensively insured. An official nationality sticker must be displayed at the rear of the vehicle, and the vehicle equipped with flares, a red breakdown-warning triangle, and a full set of spares (including bulbs).

Drive on the right, pass on the left and give way to the right, even on roundabouts. Speed limits are 120km/h (70mph) on motorways,

90km/h (55mph), or 80km (50mph) for big vans or caravans on rural roads; 50km/h (30mph) or 40km/h (25mp/h) if towing something in town. Drivers and all passengers must wear seat belts, and motorcyclists must wear helmets. Blood-alcohol limits are in line with European countries – 50mg alcohol per 100ml of blood – so just two beers will put you over the limit. Traffic control points and radar speed traps are common, particularly at the entrance to towns; foreigners, especially in rental vehicles, are likely to be waved through, but make sure the rental company has provided all required documentation in the glove box.

Petrol *(benzin)* and diesel *(mazot)* are readily available around larger towns and resorts, sometimes on a 24-hr basis; however, stations can be far apart in eastern Turkey. Petrol is available three

Durmak Yasaktır	No Stopping
Yol Yapımı	Men Working (Road Works)
Dikkat	Danger
Yavaş	Slow Down
Tek Yön	One-way
Giremez	No Entry
Şehir Merkezi	Town Centre

Some useful phrases:

Driver's licence	**Ehliyet**
Petrol	**Benzin**
Petrol station	**Benzin istasyonu**
Oil	**Motor yagi**
Tyre	**Lastik**
Brakes	**Frenler**
It does not work.	**Calismiyor.**
Fill the tank, please.	**Doldurum, lütfen.**
I've had a breakdown.	**Arabam arızalandı.**
There's been an accident.	**Bir kaza oldu.**

grades: super, normal and lead-free fuel *(kurşunsuz)*, the latter rarer in rural districts; so-called euro-diesel is more efficient than standard. In most of the country, you can pay for fuel by credit card.

E

ELECTRICITY

220V/50Hz; continental-style 2 round-pin plugs. UK Visitors will require an adapter; travellers from North America will also need a converter.

EMBASSIES AND CONSULATES

Foreign embassies are all in Ankara, but most major countries also have consulates in İstanbul and there are also some in larger resorts.
Consulates (in İstanbul unless otherwise stated)
Australia: 2nd Floor, Suzer Plaza, Asker Ocağı Cad.15, Elmadağ, tel: 0212-243 1333; **Canada:** İstiklâl Caddesi 373/5, Beyoğlu, tel: 0212-251 9838; **Ireland:** Ali Riza Gürcan Caddesi, Meridyen İş Merkezi Kat 4, no, 417, tel: 0212-482 1862; **UK:** Mesrutiyet Cad. 34, Tepebaşı, Beyoğlu, tel: 0212-293 7540; in Antalya: Gürsu Mah. 324 Sok. 6, Konyaaltı, tel: 0242-228 2811; in Bodrum: Cafer Paşa Caddesi, İkinci Emsan Evleri 7, tel: 0252-313 0021; in Fethiye, Atatürk Caddesi, Likya İş Merkezi, Kat 2, 202, tel: 0252- 614 6302; in İzmir: 1442 Sok. 49, Alsancak, tel: 0232-463 5151; and in Marmaris: Barbaros Cad. 11, tel: 0252-412 6486; **US:** Kaplıcalar Mevkii 2, İstinye, tel: 0212-335 9000.

Embassies in Ankara
Australia: Nenehatun Cad. 83, Gaziosmanpaşa, tel: 0312-459 9500; **Canada:** Cinnah Cad. 58, Çankaya, tel: 0312-409 2712; **New Zealand:** Iran Cad. 13/4, Kavaklıdere, tel: 0312-467 9054; **UK:** Şehit Ersan Cad. 46/A, Cankaya, tel: 0312-455 3344; **US:** Atatürk Bulv. 110, Kavaklıdere, tel: 0312-455 5555.

EMERGENCY NUMBERS (see also POLICE)

154 Traffic police
155 Police, general
110 Urban fire department
112 Ambulance

Help!	**Imdat!**
I am ill.	**Hastayım.**
Call a doctor.	**Doktor cagirim.**
Where is the hospital?	**Nerede hastane?**

G

GAY AND LESBIAN TRAVELLERS

Although homosexual activity between consenting adults over the age of 18 is legal, Turks are generally not accepting of gay lifestyles and it is illegal to print and distribute material promoting homosexuality. Members of the same sex travel and socialise together, Turkish men often greet each other with a (cheek) kiss and make physical contact with one another, so gay couples should feel quite comfortable travelling together. However, sexually charged contact could result in violence. Bodrum, Alanya, Antalya and Marmaris are considered the most gay-friendly resorts, though the only place with dedicated clubs is İstanbul, where the scene is centred around Beyoğlu.

GETTING THERE (see also AIRPORTS)

By air. Most international carriers fly to İstanbul. In summer, there are many additional direct flights (no-frills scheduled and charter) to the resort airports of Dalaman, Bodrum and Antalya. The national carrier, Turkish Airlines (THY, www.thy.com), provides direct services across the globe, as well as domestic services. From the UK, Thomas Cook and Thomson offer flight-only charter deals in sea-

son, and low-cost carriers such as easyJet (www.easyjet.com), Pegasus Air (www.flypgs.com), Anadolujet (www.anadolujet.com) and
Jet2 (www.jet2.com) provide flights throughout the year.

By land. Travelling from other European cities to İstanbul by train
is long (about 72 hours from London) and far more expensive than
a flight, only really worth it if you plan to make stops en route.
Through tickets from the UK are in fact no longer sold; the best single website for planning is www.seat61.com. Railpasses are of little
use in getting to Turkey – only for under-26s might a 'Global' In-
terRail pass (www.interrailnet.com) save a bit of money.

It takes up to four days to drive to Turkey from most places in
Western Europe. The most direct all-land route from the UK goes
via Belgium, Germany, Austria, Hungary and Bulgaria. Alterna-
tively, drive to Italy and then to Greece or Turkey by ferry.

By sea. Ferries currently run from both Ancona and Brindisi in Italy
to Çeşme, near İzmir – these are the last surviving seagoing links with
Europe. Marmara Lines connects Ancona with Çeşme from late May
to mid-September only, while Mesline MedEuropean Seaways links
Brindisi with Çeşme at roughly the same period; full information
available on www.cemar.it. There are also (often seasonal) services
from the Greek islands opposite to various Turkish resort-ports;
www.feribot.net is a useful information and booking resource.

GUIDES AND TOURS

Wherever you go in Turkey, you will encounter guides offering their
services outside museums or archaeological sites. Some are properly qualified, licensed and excellent at their job; others provide en-
tertainment at best. If you want a guarantee, hire a guide through
the tourist office. Fees are not high. If you are put off by a guide's
persistence, don't hire him. On the other hand, if he speaks reasonably good English and seems knowledgeable, you might take the
plunge. Don't be put off if at the end of the tour the guide offers to
take you to a relative's carpet shop – it is part of the profession.

For special-interest tours, the following agencies are recommended:

IN TURKEY
Middle Earth Travel, Göreme, Cappadocia, tel: 0384-271 2559, www.middleearthtravel.com. Hiking/trekking both locally and along Lycian/St Paul trails, plus conventional sightseeing.
Crowded House Tours, Eceabat, Gallipoli, tel: 0286-8141565, www.crowdedhousegallipoli.com. Battlefield tour operator.
AlternatifTurizm, Marmaris, tel: 0252-417 2720, www.alternatifraft. com. Main local outfitter for sea-kayaking, river-rafting, canyoning, trekking along this coast.
KirkitVoyage, Sultanahmet, İstanbul, and Avanos, Cappadocia, tel: 0212-5182282, www.kirkit.com. Mountain-biking and horse-riding in Cappadocia, plus general cultural tours.

OVERSEAS
Andante Travels (UK), tel: 01722-713800, www.andantetravels. co.uk. Up-market tours to archaeological and historical sites, led by distinugished experts.
The Imaginative Traveller (UK), tel: 0473-667 337, www. imaginative-traveller.com. Variety of escorted overland tours, many family-friendly, covering all of Turkey and visiting lesser-known spots as well as the main attractions.
Cultural Folk Tours (US), tel: 1-800-935 8875, http://culturalfolktours. com. Led by musican Bora Özkök, these 15-to-27-day tours give real insight into seldom-visited parts of Turkey.

H

HEALTH AND MEDICAL CARE
You don't need any inoculations for travel to Turkey and there are no serious health risks, although the coastal area east of Alanya does have malaria in season. The most common problems

for tourists are mild stomach upsets, sunburn and/or heat stroke in high summer, and alcohol poisoning. All are easily avoided – keep washing your hands, drink bottled water, eat only freshly cooked, hygienically prepared food; wear a hat and sunblock and drink plenty of water; and keep the alcohol levels down. Also, be careful in the countryside – there are poisonous scorpions, snakes and spiders.

Make sure you have full travel insurance that will cover any medical treatment you may need. You may be asked to pay for treatment upfront, so keep all receipts. Pharmacies are well stocked, and can treat many minor ailments; emergency after-hour locations are posted in all pharmacies. Your hotel will be able to get you a doctor if necessary. The quality of medical care is generally good.

Water. Tap water is heavily chlorinated and not exactly tasty (in İstanbul it is absolutely to be avoided). Turks prefer inexpensive bottled water; still water is *şişe suyu*, sparkling water is *maden suyu*. Rural springs are labelled *içilir*, *içibelir* or *içme suyu* (all meaning 'drinkable') or *içilmez* ('not drinkable').

Where can I find a doctor/ dentist?	**Nereden bir doktor/ bir disci bulabilirim?**
Where is the nearest pharmacy?	**En yakin eczane nerededir?**
Sunburn	**Güneş yanğı**
Fever	**Ateş**
Stomach ache	**Mide bozulması**

L

LANGUAGE

While English is spoken widely in hotels and other tourist facilities, you may well find yourself in many places in Turkey where English is unknown. Try to have at least a few words of Turkish up your sleeve: English-speaking or not, Turks will applaud your efforts.

Among Atatürk's sweeping reforms were his attempts to 'modernise' the Turkish language. As a result, since 1929 Turkish has been written in a modified Roman alphabet. Many letters are pronounced as they are in English. Some exceptions:

c like **j** in **j**am
ç like **ch** in **ch**ip
ğ almost silent, lengthening the preceding vowel
h always pronounced
ı like the sound between b and l in 'probable'
j like **s** in plea**s**ure
ö like **ur** in f**ur**
ş like **sh** in **sh**ell
ü like **ew** in f**ew**

Some basic words and phrases:

Good morning	**Günaydın**	Goon-eye-DEN
Please	**Lütfen**	LEWT-fen
Thank you	**Teşekkür ederim**	Tay-shake-kur eh-day-REEM
Bon appetit	**Afiyet olsun**	
Cheers!	**Şerefe!**	
Excuse me	**Ozur dilerim**	Oh-ZEWR deel-air-eem
Where is...?	**Nerde...?**	NEH-deer...?
I don't understand	**Anlamıyorum**	Ahn-LAH-muh-yohr-um
I'd like...	**Istiyorum...**	EES-tee-yohr-ruhm
How much is that?	**Bu ne kadar?**	boo neh kaddar?
Is there a toilet here?	**Tuvalet var mı?**	
OK	**Tamam**	
Yes/No	**Evet/Hayır**	

Numbers:

one	**bir**	beer
two	**iki**	ee-KEE
three	**üc**	ooch
four	**dört**	doort
five	**beş**	besh
six	**altı**	ahl-TUH
seven	**yedi**	YED-dee
eight	**sekiz**	sek-KEEZ
nine	**dokuz**	doh-KOOZ
ten	**on**	ohn
hundred	**yüz**	yewz

Days of the week:

Monday	**Pazartesi**	Pahz-AHR-teh-see
Tuesday	**Salı**	SAHL-luh
Wednesday	**Çarşamba**	Char-shahm-BAH
Thursday	**Perşembe**	Pair-shem-BAH
Friday	**Cuma**	JOON-ahz
Saturday	**Cumartesi**	Joom-AHR-teh-see
Sunday	**Pazar**	Pahz-AHR

M

MAPS

Most town tourist offices can provide a reasonable town plan, but good country or regional maps are hard to find. Consider buying one before you leave home; the best currently available overseas is Reise Know-How's 1:700,000-scale Western Turkey Mediterranean Coast and Cyprus, which covers the entire southern and western third of the country. Locally, Sabri Aydal's 1:250,000 products for Lycia, Cappadocia and Pamphylia are available.

MEDIA

Some foreign English-language newspapers are available from news-stands in İstanbul and in larger resorts. The two local English-language dailies are the Hürriyet Daily News and the Today's Zaman. News in English is broadcast on CNN, BBC World and Al Jazeera; the better hotels offer a satellite package including these, as well as the private Digitürk network's English-language CNBC-e and E2 channels.

MONEY

Currency. The unit of currency is the Türk Lirası (TL, Turkish Lira); 1TL is broken into 100 kuruş, which are available in coins of 5, 10, 25 and 50 kuruş, plus 1 TL. Notes come in denominations of 5, 10, 20, 50, 100 and 200TL.

Most travellers obtain cash either through the ubiquitous ATMs, or exchange sterling, euro or US$ bills at dedicated foreign-exchange booths (*döviz burolar*); these are open much longer hours than banks, and charge no commision, though usually offer a poorer rate. Credit/debit cards are useful for air ticket and petrol purchase; most brands are accepted. Payment in foreign currency is happily accepted for purchase of valuable souvenirs (eg carpets).

OPENING TIMES

In general, hours are: archaeological sites, 8.30am–6.30pm daily in summer (with many variations); government offices, 8.30am–12.30pm and 1.30–5.30pm, Mon–Fri (tourist offices are often open on weekends too during summer); museums, 8.30/9am–5.30/6pm Tues–Sun (with many variations); restaurants, noon–2.30 or 3pm for lunch, 7 or 7.30pm–10 or 10.30pm for dinner (those that have music and offer drinks will often remain open longer); shops, 9am–7pm (as late as midnight during the summer season in some resorts).

P

POLICE *(polis)*

There are many kinds of police in Turkey. Municipal *polis* deal with petty crime, traffic, parking and other day-to-day matters; the *Jandarma*, a better trained national force, actually a branch of the army, handle serious crime and civil unrest; *Trafik Polis* monitor town streets and highways; the *Belediye Zabitası* (market police) patrol market areas with an eye out for shoplifters and dishonest merchants; and the *Turizm Polis*, who often speak English, are on hand in busy tourist areas.

POST OFFICES

Turkish post offices are easily recognised by their PTT signs. In the major cities and resorts, the central post office is open 8am–midnight; others are open 8.30am–12.30pm and 1.30–5.30pm. Express service is faster but much more expensive than standard post; most people use courier companies for anything precious. Post offices also offer metered counter-telephone service.

PUBLIC HOLIDAYS

Turks enjoy year-round festivals *(see page 141)*, and observe the following nation-wide holidays:

1 January	New Year's Day
23 April	National Independence and Children's Day
19 May	Atatürk Commemoration and Youth and Sports Day
30 August	Victory Day
29 October	Republic Day (anniversary of the declaration of the Turkish Republic)
10 November	Anniversary of Atatürk's death

The most important Islamic holidays, which drift backward 11 days annually relative to the western calendar, are Şeker Bayramı (end of Ramazan), falling in mid-summer until 2015, and Kurban Bayramı (Festival of the Sacrifice), occurring lately in mid-autumn. Both are multi-day festivals, and the country effectively shuts down for the duration as everyone who can goes on holiday. Many restaurants close during Ramazan at midday, except in tourist resorts.

R

RELIGION

Turkey is 99 percent Muslim. In İstanbul and İzmir, you will find Jewish, Armenian, Catholic and Greek Orthodox services. Non-Muslims are welcome to visit mosques, though often not during prayers. Visitors must remove their shoes (at larger mosques, an attendant will check them; elsewhere, there's a rack inside the door on which to place them). Men and women should cover their legs and upper arms (no shorts or sleeveless T-shirts) and women should cover their heads, shoulders and knees.

T

TELEPHONE (telefon)

Turkey's mobile phone networks offer widespread coverage; they use the European operating system, so North Americans will need a tri-band phone. Foreign visitors should not roam on their home SIM for anything other than texting; since Turkish networks are not subject to EU roaming caps, making or receiving voice calls is extortionately expensive. Instead, purchase a local pay-as-you-go SIM card (they start from around 20TL) or, for somewhat dearer rates, an international roaming SIM card (www.gosim.co.uk).

Because of the prevalence of mobile use, there are fewer public phones now. They are usually blue, and take phone cards (from post offices and newsstands) or credit cards. Instructions are available in several languages. For more quiet, go to a TT (Türk Telekom) premises. Local calls are quite cheap. To call internationally, dial 00, then the country code. Calling Turkey from abroad, its country code is 90; omit the initial zero of the 11-digit Turkish land or mobile number. Avoid phoning from your hotel room, as surcharges are horrendous.

TIME ZONES

Turkey is 2 hours ahead of Greenwich Mean Time (GMT), which places it 2 hours ahead of London, 7 hours ahead of New York, 10 hours ahead of Los Angeles, 2 hours behind Johannesburg, 9 hours behind Sydney, and 11 hours behind Auckland. Turkey observes Daylight Savings Time as in Europe: 1 hour forward the last Sunday in March, reverting to standard time the last Sunday in October.

New York	London	**Turkey**	Sydney	Los Angeles
5am	10am	**noon**	8pm	2am

TIPPING

Tips provide many Turks working in tourism with a good share of their income. Tip bellhops about 2TL a bag, and leave about 1TL per day of your stay for a hotel chambermaid. In many small hotels and *pansiyons*, the desk staff does double duty as cleaners, room service attendants, breakfast waiters and all-around service providers, and it is nice to leave a generous tip upon departure. To tip a taxi driver, simply round up the total. Tour guides and excursion-boat operators usually also expect a tip; 15–25TL per day of friendly service is appropriate. In non-fancy restaurants where no service charge or *garsoniye* ('waiter charge') is levied, 5 to 10 percent of the bill is fine; in fancier places, mandatory service charges can approach 20 percent of the bill, but leave a bit more on top if service has been good.

TOILETS *(tuvalet)*

There are plenty of public toilets, with most cafés and restaurants, petrol stations and tourist sights having facilities. They are often kept clean by a full-time warden, who will charge users up to 1TL. Most offer a mix of Western-style and Turkish squat toilets. All have little squirter-pipes aimed your nether parts, as local custom requires cleansing with running water. Carry a bit of toilet paper with you to blot yourself dry, and (usually) deposit this in a basket next to the basin, not in it. The gents' toilet is designated by *baylar*, the ladies' by *bayanlar*.

TOURIST INFORMATION

The official Turkish tourism websites are www.goturkey.com, www.tourismturkey.org and www.gototurkey.co.uk. Turkish Tourist Offices abroad:

UK: 4th Floor, 29-30 St James' Street, London SW1A 1HB, tel: 020-7839 7778

US: 821 United Nations Plaza, New York, NY 10017, tel: 212-687-2194

Tourist offices in Turkey:

Ankara: Gazi Mustafa Kemal Bulvarı 121, 06570 Maltepe, tel: 0312-229 2631

İstanbul: At Meydanı, Sultanahmet, tel:0212-518 1802/518 8754

İzmir: 1344 Sokak 2, Passport, tel: 0232-483 5117

There are also variably helpful offices in Alanya, Antakya, Antalya, Avanos, Ayvalık, Bodrum, Bursa, Çanakkale, Çeşme, Edirne, Fethiye, Gaziantep, Kaş, Konya, Kuşadası, Marmaris and Selçuk.

TRANSPORT

A good public transport network makes it relatively easy to move between major cities and towns in Turkey without a car. Even some remote archaeological sites and beaches may be reached by public transport, but service can be infrequent.

Any town of any size has at least one *otogar* (bus station) that is the hub of local and long-distance transport. Long-distance buses, many of which travel by night, are often the only mode of transport available between cities and towns. Better companies, worth paying extra for, include Ulusoy, Varan, Metro, Pamukkale and Kamil Koç.

Large towns and cities are served by local buses; buy tickets at kiosks before boarding, though in İstanbul most are now geared only for swiping of electronic, reloadable tickets called *akbil*. İstanbul, Ankara and İzmir all have efficient, if often limited, metro networks. İstanbul, of course, has an extensive ferry network along the Bosphorus, and there are also useful car ferries and sea-buses across the Sea of Marmara.

Dolmuş fleets (often vans) also operate in most towns, and can serve as the main transport between smaller villages off major bus routes as well. They ply will drop off passengers upon request along the way. Stops are marked with a 'D'. In resorts, a *dolmuş* often provides fast and inexpensive transport to a beach or nearby archaeological site.

Numerous yellow taxis serve larger towns; make sure the meter is running and visible, and that the driver understands where it is you want to go (write it down to save problems). For trips to remote sites, it is worth doing a flat-rate deal for the morning or day, including waiting time, so you will have return transport.

Trains of interest to tourists are mostly confined to the triangle İstanbul-İzmir-Ankara; the best ones are cheaper than buses, more comfortable, and sometimes faster.

When is the next bus to…?	**Bir sonraki otobüs kaçta kalkiyor…?**
A ticket to…	**a bir bilet…**
What time does it leave?	**Kaçta kalkiyor?**
How long does it take?	**Ne kadar surebilir?**
How much does it cost?	**Ne kadar?**

Domestic flights are numerous, serve an increasing number of hitherto obscure airports and can be surprisingly cheap. In addition to THY, Anadolujet and Pegasus *(see page 166)*, Atlas Jet (www.atlasjet.com), Sun Express (www.sunexpress.com) and Onurair (www.onurair.com.tr) provide internal services.

▼

VISAS AND ENTRY REQUIREMENTS

Tourist visa requirements and costs vary substantially according to your nationality. All travellers need a passport valid for at least six months. Visas for 90 days are usually granted on entry and in the case of the US and Uk the fee is £10/$US20.

Turkish regulations permit visitors to bring all personal effects, including one camera, one music system (eg iPod), one personal computer and one video player. Duty-free import limits for luxury consumables include 5 litres of wine or spirits, 200 cigarettes, 50 cigars, and 200g of tobacco, 1.5kg coffee, 500g of tea and 1kg of chocolate. Exiting Turkey into the EU (particularly Greece), there is a duty-free limit for souvenir purchases. It is an offence to attempt to export 'antiquities', whose exact definition is vague but can include very old carpets. Reputable dealers will prepare a document for you stating that the purchased item is not an antiquity.

Currency Restrictions and VAT. There is no limit on the amount of foreign currency you can bring into Turkey, but sums above $US15,000 equivalent should be declared. Do not bring significant amounts of Turkish lira – you always get a better rate inside the country.

A variable (8 to 23 percent) value-added tax (KDV in Turkish) is added to most purchases in Turkey. Non-EU-resident foreigners can claim a VAT refund on departure providing they have dealt with retailers who furnished them with a Special VAT Refund Invoice. In practice, only the most expensive shops participate in the scheme, and it's not worth pursuing except for very high-value souvenirs.

WEBSITES AND INTERNET ACCESS

www.biletix.com Booking for arts, music and sporting events, mostly in İstanbul and Ankara.

www.turkeytravelplanner.com American-orientated site with loads of practical tips and links to vetted service providers.

www.trekkinginturkey.com Information on major trekking areas and marked long-distance routes, with on-line sales of guides and maps.

www.turkeycentral.com Useful portal with links to a variety of sites.

www.tulumba.com New-York-based shopping site specialising in all things Turkish, especially foodstuffs and music.

www.mymerhaba.com Aimed at long-term residents, and strongest on İstanbul, but wide-ranging and authoritative, with good events listings.

www.boutiqueandsmallhotels.com A good directory of characterful hotels, across the entire country.

Turkey must be one of the most wired-up (or rather, wire-less) societies in the world. Wi-Fi zones are ubiquitous in bars and restaurants, and even surprisingly modest *pansiyons* will have a signal (usually free), in common areas if not every room; luxury hotels are more apt to charge for use.

YOUTH HOSTELS

Pansiyons in Turkey are so reasonably priced that hostels per se are restricted to backpacker meccas such as İstanbul, Kuşadası, Fethiye, Çanakkale and Köyceğiz. Along the Lycian coast, interesting adaptations of these – arisen to get around a ban on 'permanent' buildings in protected areas – are the so-called 'treehouse' lodges, particularly at Olympos, near Ölüdeniz and elsewhere along the Lycian Way.

Recommended Hotels

Our selection of hotels includes only those that we believe will in some way enhance your stay. They may have great character, be well located, provide excellent value, or be unusually well equipped with amenities. Reservations are essential in better hotels almost anywhere in high season, and are highly recommended at other times.

The symbols below indicate the price range for a double room with bath, including breakfast. However, prices may vary with the season.

$$$$$	above £200 ($320)
$$$$	£130–200 ($210–320)
$$$	£75–130 ($130–210)
$$	£50–75 ($80–130)
$	below £50 ($80)

İSTANBUL AND SURROUNDINGS

Anemon Galata $$$$ *Büyükhendek Cad. 11, Kuledibi, Galata, tel: 0212-293 2343, www.anemonhotels.com.* One of the only special hotels in the new city, the Anemon is intimate, beautifully decorated and perfectly positioned within easy walking distance of Beyoğlu nightlife. The rooftop bar and restaurant has superb views across the Bosphorus and Golden Horn to the old city. 23 rooms and seven suites.

Çirağan Palace Kempinski $$$$$ *Çirağan Cad. 32, Beşiktaş, 34349 İstanbul, tel: 0212-326 4646, www.kempinski-istanbul.com.* The most luxurious hotel in İstanbul occupies the grounds of a palace built for the last of the Ottoman sultans on the Bosphorus. Only 12 opulent suites occupy the original palace; the other 295 standard rooms and 15 suites face the Bosphorus-side gardens and swimming pool from a new wing. Spa and two gourmet restaurants on-site.

Four Seasons Hotel Sultanahmet $$$$$ *Tevkifhane Sok. 1, Sultanahmet, İstanbul 34110, tel: 0212-402 3000, www.fourseasons.*

com/istanbul/. One of the most elegant hotels in İstanbul is also one of the most unusual – it occupies a former prison. The 65 rooms and suites, beautifully appointed with kilims and handsome furniture and equipped with lovely baths, face the former prison yard or look out on the Sea of Marmara. Glass-roofed restaurant and health club.

Empress Zoë \$\$\$ *Akbıyık Cad. 4/1, Sultanahmet, 34122 İstanbul, tel: 0212-518 4360, www.emzoe.com.* The charms of the textiles-filled interior and of the American owner, Ann Nevans, make this small hotel a favourite with return visitors. All rooms, reached by a narrow spiral staircase that may be an obstacle to some travellers, are comfortable, but best is the penthouse, with its large terrace and stunning views. 22 rooms and three suites, distributed over four structures.

Pera Palace \$\$\$\$ *Meşrutiyet Cad. 52, Tepebaşi, 80050 İstanbul, tel: 0212-377 4000, www.perapalas.com.* Istanbul's oldest hotel was built in 1892 to billet arriving Orient Express passengers, and the decor and graciousness of those days still prevail. It has emerged from a complete 2008–10 refurbishment with four-star standards (including spa and gym) but its retro atmosphere intact.

Sarı Konak \$\$\$\$ *Mimar Mehmet Ağa Cad. 42–46, Sultanahmet, İstanbul 34122, tel: 0212-638 6258, www.istanbulhotelsarikonak. com.* Ottoman-restoration hotels seem to be opening all the time in Sultanahmet, but this establishment run by two brothers remains one of the best. The 17 rooms and suites are simply but stylishly furnished, and many look over the Sea of Marmara. The finest views, though, are from the rooftop terrace, where snacks and drinks are served; breakfast is given in an old courtyard.

Sumahan on the Water \$\$\$\$ *Kuleli Cad. 51, Çengelköy, İstanbul 34684, tel: 0216-422 8000 www.sumahan.com.* A former *rakı* factory on the Asian shore of the Bosphorus magnificently converted into a small designer hotel with some of the finest views in the world, fabulously chic décor, a fitess centre, spa and hamam on site, plus one of the city's best seafood restaurants. A private boat links the hotel with the European shore. 18 rooms and suites.

Yeşil Ev $$$ *Kabasakal Cad. 5, Sultanahmet, İstanbul 34122, tel: 0212-517 6786, www.yesilev.com.tr.* Rebuilt former mansion on a quiet street near the sights of the old city. The 18 units vary in size, so ask for one of the larger ones; all are decorated with old bedsteads and other unique furnishings. Most face a leafy rear garden; the one suite has its own Turkish bath.

PRINCES ISLANDS

Splendid Palas $$ *23 Nisan Cad. 53, Büryükada 81330, tel: 0216-382 6950, www.splendidhotel.net.* For an atmospheric retreat from İstanbul, look no further than this wooden, 19th-century inn set in lovely poolside gardens on the largest island of the archipelago. Guest rooms are very large, and what they lack in modern amenities, they make up for with lovely old furnishings and plenty of Victorian-resort atmosphere. 70 rooms and four suites.

EDIRNE

Taşodalar $$$ *Hamam Sok. 3, behind Selimiye Camii, 22800 Edirne, tel: 0284-213 1404, www.tasodalar.com.tr.* The town's quietest (and newest) boutique hotel, this stone-built 15th-century structure is ideal for families and drivers with its private, secure carpark. Nine rooms sport dark-wood floors and trim, though other decor mixes genuine antiques with kitsch; upstairs units have mosque views.

SEA OF MARMARA AND AEGEAN COAST

ASSOS (BEHRAMKALE)

Biber Evi $$$$ *Behramkale square, tel: 0286-721 7410, www.biberevi.com.* Peppers (*biberler*) are the theme here – 20 types in the garden, and pepper-portraying tiles in the 6 units. Ceilings and cabinetry are carved from salvaged Black Sea wood; the fireplace-lounge-bar is the big winter hit, though the upper terrace is the *pièce de resistance*. Host Lütfi is a font of local lore. Half-board obligatory in season – no great sorrow, as village restaurants are undistinguished.

BODRUM AND ENVIRONS

Lavanta Hotel $$$$ *Yalıkavak 48430, tel: 0252-385 2167, www.lavanta.com.* Crowded Bodrum seems far away from this delightful retreat set in gardens overlooking relatively unspoilt Yalıkavak bay. The airy, wood-floored units all have terraces and some antique furnishings; home-cooked meals are served in a lovely dining room or on the terrace by the large pool. 8 rooms and 7 remote, self-catering 'residences', these also let by the week. Open May 15–Oct 15.

Karia Princess $$$$$ *Myndos Cad 8, Eskiçeşme Mahallesi, Bodrum 48400, tel: 0252-316 8971 www.kariaprincess.com.* Probably the best town-centre accommodation. Although within walking distance of the busy waterfront, it feels quiet and secluded. A classy place capable of hosting weddings; its Turkish bath is one of the best you'll see along the Aegean coast. Open all year.

BURSA

Çelik Palas $$$$$ *Çekirge Cad. 79, Bursa 16070, tel: 0224-233 3800, www.celikpalasotel.com.* Built in the 1930s on the express orders of Atatürk, this five-star hotel was comprehensively gutted and rebuilt over 18 months from 2009, and can now claim to be the best accommodation in Bursa's baths district. Its hamam is one of the most sumptuous in Turkey; there's also a huge, dedicated conference centre. 141 units, including 21 suites.

ÇANAKKALE

Kervansaray $$$ *Fetvane Sok 13, tel: 0286-217 8192, www.anzachotel.com/kervansaray.htm.* Justifiably popular hotel installed in a 1903-vintage judge's mansion and a rear annexe. Best of the mansion rooms with their mock Belle-Époque furnishings are no. 206 or 207, overlooking the garden with its single free-standing suite. Less distinguished are the annexe rooms, upstairs from the breakfast area serving above-average starts to the day.

ÇEŞME

Taş Otel $$$$ *Kemalpaşa Cad. 132, Alaçatı, tel: 0232-716 7772, www.tasotel.com*. This former Greek village near Çeşme must now have at least a dozen restoration inns of boutique calibre; Taş, installed in an 1890s-built mansion, was the first and still about the best. Breakfast is served on a terrace overlooking the lawn-set pool; just 7 rooms, so bookings – especially at weekends – are mandatory. Open all year.

İZMIR

Beyond $$$–$$$$ *1376 Cad. 5, İzmir, tel: 0232-463 0585, www.hotelbeyond.com*. One of a crop of boutique hotels opening in İzmir, this trendy place, right in the city centre near the seafront, makes slightly disconcerting use of six different colour palettes in the rooms (all in the name of Chakra therapy), but is stylish, comfortable and has plentiful amenities for business travellers, including a good restaurant. 60 rooms and suites.

KUŞADASI

Club Caravanserail $$ *Atatürk Bulv. 2, Kuşadası 09400, tel: 0256-614 4115*. An atmospheric inn lodged in a kervansaray dating from 1618. The courtyard shelters a lovely garden and 26 rooms (plus 1 suite) sport polished wood floors, fireplaces, kilims and other textiles. May be noisy when tacky 'Turkish Nights' staged in the courtyard, but still good value. Open Mar–Nov.

Kismet $$$ *Gazi Beğendi Bulv. 1, Turkmen Mah., Kuşadası 09400, tel: 0256-618 1290, www.kismet.com.tr*. Originally built in 1966 by Princess Hümeyra Özbaş (1917–2000), a granddaughter of the last sultan, this venerable self-contained resort set on its own peninsula is still run by her descendants. Because

of the Ottoman dynastic connection, royalty and leadership of
many states, and various domestic celebrities, have stopped in,
but it's not hopelessly snooty; the 108 rooms and suites are airy
and unpretentious, plus there's a large pool. Open all year.

PAMUKKALE

Colossae Thermal $$$$ *Karahayıt, Denizli, tel: 0258-271 4156,
www.colossaehotel.com.* The village on the plateau behind Pamukkale has been completely overtaken by large resort hotels, all
with spas, taking advantage of the hot springs. This is one of the
best, with two pools, several restaurants and a full health and fit-
ness centre. 231 units, including 21 suites.

SELÇUK

Kalehan $$ *North end of main through road (Highway 550), Selçuk
35920, tel: 0232-892 6154, www.kalehan.com.* Highest-standard
hotel in Selçuk, with antique and mock-Ottoman decor wedded to
58 modern units, and a competent restaurant for sustenance after
a day at the ruins. Extensive garden and pool, with views up to the
castle just behind. Easy parking, but set back enough from the high-
way to minimize noise. Open all year.

MEDITERRANEAN COAST

ANTALYA

Mediterra Art $$ *Zafer Sok. 5, Kaleiçi, Antalya, tel: 0242-244
8624, www.mediterraarthotel.com.* Three carefully restored Ot-
toman houses within the walls of old Kaleiçi comprise this 2008-
opened boutique hotel furnished with gleaming wood, exposed
stone pointing and rugs. Courtyard pool, indoor and outdoor
restaurants and bar. 21 rooms and suites.

Özmen Pansiyon $ *Zeytin Çıkmazı 5, Kaleiçi, tel: 0242-241
6505, www.ozmenpension.com.* Cheap and cheerful yet well-

managed pansiyon with a great roof terrace right in the heart of the old town. Open all year; competitively priced airport transfers available. 25 rooms.

DALYAN

Dalyan Resort $$$–$$$$ *Kaunos Sok. 50, Maraş Mah., Dalyan 48840, tel: 0252-284 5499, www.dalyanresort.com.* Self-contained riverside complex that's the town's most comfortable digs, with four grades of tasteful, travertine-tiled units, an airy domed restaurant, rental canoes and a hamam with mud therapy offered. It's popular with package operators, and claims to be open all year.

KALKAN

Lizo Hotel $ *Milli Egemenlik Caddesi, Kalamar Yolu 57, Pk 110 Kalkan, tel: 0242-844 3381, http://lizohotel.com.* Small, family-run hotel at the back of the town, with restaurant, bar, garden and pool. Great views, friendly service and excellent food make this a firm favourite, in spite of the steep walk back after dinner or the beach.

KAŞ

Gardenia Otel $$$ *Hükümet Cad. 47, Küçükçakıl, Kaş 07580, tel: 0242-836 1618, www.gardeniahotel-kas.com.* The most ambitious boutique hotel in Kaş has just 11 varied rooms and suites distributed over four floors, their Philippe Starck decor and marble floors juxtaposed with somewhat garish art in the common areas. The proprietors speak perfect American English. Buffet breakfast to 11am; no children under 12.

Hideway Hotel $$ *Eski Kilise Arkası 7, tel: 0242-836 1887, www.hotelhideaway.com.* Thoroughly refurbished since 2008, this is the most attractive mid-range option in town, with especially airy third-floor rooms and a pricier luxe jacuzzi suite. Common areas include a small plunge pool, a TV-lounge-cum-library, and a stunning rooftop restaurant with homestyle cooking. Very outgoing, multilingual Belgian-Turkish hosts; credit cards accepted. Open all year.

PATARA (GELEMİŞ)

Patara Viewpoint $ *Top of east ridge road, Gelemiş, tel: 0242-843 5184 or 0533-350 0347, www.pataraviewpoint.com.* Long-established hotel in an unbeatable setting, American-style wall showers in the bathrooms, a pool-bar where breakfast is served, and a cushioned, Turkish-style night-time terrace with fireplace. Advantageous weekly rates; credit cards accepted. Open March–Nov.

SIDE

Beach House $ *Barbaros Caddesi, tel: 0242-753 1607, www.beachhouse-hotel.com.* Small, friendly hotel with airy balconied rooms overlooking Side's eastern beach. The resort's first (1965) lodgings, it has plenty of character but is also very well run by an Australian-Turkish couple; there's an affiliated restaurant run by their son.

CAPPADOCIA AND CENTRAL ANATOLIA

ANKARA

Angora House Hotel $$ *Kalekapısı Sok. 16–18, Hisar, Ankara 06240, tel: 0312-309 8380.* One of the very few small boutique hotels in this business-orientated city, this charmingly restored Ottoman house within the citadel has just six unique rooms with carved-wood ceilings, quality bedding, antiques and rugs. Walking distance to most attractions; helpful English-speaking proprietor.

GÖREME

Kelebek $–$$$ *Aydınlı Mah., Yavuz Sok. 1, Göreme 50180, tel: 0384-271 2531, www.kelebekhotel.com.* Magnificent views, a small outdoor pool, a cute hamam and a range of impeccable rooms to suit all budgets make this spot a winner. Some of the 31 units are cut out of fairy chimneys or installed in old caves; others are in the original stone-built house.

GÜZELYURT (GELVERİ)

Karballa $ *Güzelyurt 68500, tel: 0382-451 2103, www.karballa hotel.com.* This beautiful, large village just east of the Ihlara Valley is much less frequented than those in Cappadocia proper. At its centre stands this 19th-century monastery, now converted to a comfortable hotel. Most of the 20 rooms occupy the vaulted monks' cells and are galleried, with a sitting area on one level and a sleeping loft above. Good meals are served in the former refectory, and a swimming pool occupies one end of the tree-shaded gardens.

ÜÇHİSAR

Les Maisons de Cappadoce $$$$–$$$$$ *Belediye Meyd. 6, Üçhisar 50240; tel: 0384-219 2782, www.cappadoce.com.* These 16 carefully restored village houses, sleeping two to six, form a luxurious retreat ideal for families and small groups. They are equipped with kitchens, tastefully furnished and set in beautiful gardens; a gardener tends to your private patch of greenery and the management stocks your fridge before you arrive.

ÜRGÜP

Esbelli Evi $$$ *Esbelli Sok. 8, Ürgüp 50400, tel: 0384-341 3995, www.esbelli.com.tr.* The cave-hotel that kick-started the restoration and conversion movement in Cappdocia is still among the very best, with ten enormous suites, a vaulted, Ottoman-style lounge perfect for having a drink with new friends, and an array of pretty gardens or courtyards. Owner Suha Ersoz prides himself on offering a home-from-home service to guests.

Serinn House $$$ *Esbelli Sok. 36 Ürgüp, tel: 0384-341 6076, www.serinnhouse.com.* Run with immense charm by well-travelled Eren Serpen and designed ultra-stylishly by Turkish architect Riftat Ergör, this tiny cave-hotel (with only five rooms) brings İstanbul chic to Cappadocia. The terrace views are superb, the minimalist furnishings surprisingly compatible with troglodytic contours, and the breakfasts excellent.

EASTERN TURKEY

ANTAKYA

Savon Hotel $$ *Kurtuluş Cad. 192, tel: 0326-214 6355, www. savonhotel.com.tr.* This Ottoman soap and olive-oil factory from 1860 was converted into a boutique hotel in 2001. The stone-built building offers an original architectural background to eclectic (for which read plush) decoration for the 36 rooms and seven suites arrayed around a courtyard; a vaulted restaurant serves Turkish and Italian food, plus there's a fireplace bar.

GAZİANTEP

Anadolu Evleri $$$ *Koroğlu Sok. 6, Nemrut Dağı, tel: 0342-220 9525, www.anadoluevleri.com.* Perhaps the most tastefully restored and converted of Gaziantep's old-house boutique hotels, with its 10 high-ceilinged rooms and three suites grouped around a courtyard with adjoining bar. Walking distance to the castle and museum.

NEMRUT DAĞI

Kervansaray Nemrut $$ *Karadut Köyü, Nemrut Dağı, tel: 0416-737 2190, www.nemrutkervansaray.com.* A proper hotel on the slopes of the mountain, 8km (5 miles) from the summit in the area's highest (1,245m) village, this is the best place to spend the night if you want to see the sunrise from the mountain top. Rooms and restaurant are simple but adequate, there's a swimming pool and camping is allowed.

ŞANLIURFA

Cevahir Konak Evi $$$ *Selahattin Eyyubi Camii Karşısı, Vali Fuat Bey Caddesi, Urfa, tel: 0414-215 9377, www.cevahirkonukevi.com.* This courtyarded stone building has been converted into the city's top boutique hotel with exemplary taste (but also proper bathrooms with stall showers). Waling distance to all attractions; during summer there are *sira geceleri* (banquets with musical accompaniment) Wednesday, Friday and Saturday on the premises.

INDEX

Berlitz pocket guide

Turkey

Fifth Edition 2012

Written by Stephen Brewer
Updated by Marc Dubin
Edited by Tony Halliday
Series Editor: Tom Stainer

No part of this book may be reproduced, stored in a retrieval system or transmitted in any form or means electronic, mechanical, photocopying, recording or otherwise, without prior written permission from Berlitz Publishing. Brief text quotations with use of photographs are exempted for book review purposes only.

Every effort has been made to provide accurate information in this publication, but changes are inevitable. The publisher cannot be responsible for any resulting loss, inconvenience or injury.

All Rights Reserved
© 2012 Apa Publications (UK) Limited
Printed by CTPS-China

Berlitz Trademark Reg. U.S. Patent Office and other countries. Marca Registrada. Used under licence from the Berlitz Investment Corporation

Photography credits
akg-images/Cameraphoto 19; akg-images/Eric Lessing 21; Pete Bennett/APA 56, 93, 114, 116; Michael Coupe 95; Rebecca Erol/APA 2MR, 3BL, 4TL, 18, 29, 35, 37, 38, 42, 44, 45, 47, 48, 51, 53, 54, 119, 126, 129, 130, 135, 139, 143, 144; Tony Halliday/APA 24, 32, 36, 38, 50; iStockphoto 31; Frank Noon/APA 2M, 3ML, 3TL, 3TR, 4–5, 4BL, 4BM, 5BL, 5BR, 5TL, 5TR, 6B, 6M, 7B/137, 7M, 7T, 10, 11, 12, 16, 61, 62, 67, 68, 70, 72, 74, 75, 77, 79, 80, 81, 83, 85, 87, 89, 94, 97, 98, 99, 100, 102, 103, 105, 107, 108, 109, 111, 121, 122, 123, 124, 133, 142, 145, 146; Superstock 6T/26; Turkish Tourism 4TR, 23; Marcus Wilson-Smith/APA 64, 86, 90; Phil Wood/APA 15, 112, 113, 115, 117.

Cover picture: 4Corners Images

Contact us

At Berlitz we strive to keep our guides as accurate and up to date as possible, but if you find anything that has changed, or if you have any suggestions on ways to improve this guide, then we would be delighted to hear from you.

Berlitz Publishing, PO Box 7910,
London SE1 1WE, England.
email: berlitz@apaguide.co.uk
www.berlitzpublishing.com